Module
8

Urban Mission

Evangelism & Spiritual Warfare

Spiritual Warfare:

BINDING OF THE STRONG MAN

· ·

Evangelism:

THE CONTENT OF THE GOOD NEWS OF THE KINGDOM

· ·

Evangelism:

METHODS TO REACH THE URBAN COMMUNITY

· ·

Follow-Up and Incorporation

Capstone Module 8: Evangelism and Spiritual Warfare Student Workbook

ISBN: 978-1-62932-008-3

Contents

About the Instructor

Rev. Dr. Don L. Davis is the Executive Director of The Urban Ministry Institute and a Senior Vice President of World Impact. He attended Wheaton College and Wheaton Graduate School, and graduated summa cum laude in both his B.A. (1988) and M.A. (1989) degrees, in Biblical Studies and Systematic Theology, respectively. He earned his Ph.D. in Religion (Theology and Ethics) from the University of Iowa School of Religion.

As the Institute's Executive Director and World Impact's Senior Vice President, he oversees the training of urban missionaries, church planters, and city pastors, and facilitates training opportunities for urban Christian workers in evangelism, church growth, and pioneer missions. He also leads the Institute's extensive distance learning programs and facilitates leadership development efforts for organizations and denominations like Prison Fellowship, the Evangelical Free Church of America, and the Church of God in Christ.

A recipient of numerous teaching and academic awards, Dr. Davis has served as professor and faculty at a number of fine academic institutions, having lectured and taught courses in religion, theology, philosophy, and biblical studies at schools such as Wheaton College, St. Ambrose University, the Houston Graduate School of Theology, the University of Iowa School of Religion, the Robert E. Webber Institute of Worship Studies. He has authored a number of books, curricula, and study materials to equip urban leaders, including *The Capstone Curriculum*, TUMI's premiere sixteen-module distance education seminary instruction, *Sacred Roots: A Primer on Retrieving the Great Tradition*, which focuses on how urban churches can be renewed through a rediscovery of the historic orthodox faith, and *Black and Human: Rediscovering King as a Resource for Black Theology and Ethics*. Dr. Davis has participated in academic lectureships such as the Staley Lecture series, renewal conferences like the Promise Keepers rallies, and theological consortiums like the University of Virginia Lived Theology Project Series. He received the Distinguished Alumni Fellow Award from the University of Iowa College of Liberal Arts and Sciences in 2009. Dr. Davis is also a member of the Society of Biblical Literature, and the American Academy of Religion.

Introduction to the Module

Greetings, in the strong name of Jesus Christ!

Evangelism is proclaiming and demonstrating to the world that God has visited the world in the person of Jesus of Nazareth, and that this visitation is now accompanied by liberation from the devil and from the effects of sin! To evangelize is to prophesy deliverance in Messiah Jesus.

The lessons of this module are organized to provide you with a solid overview of the critical issues arising from a biblical grasp of evangelism and spiritual warfare. The first lesson, *Spiritual Warfare: Binding of the Strong Man*, outlines the war of the universe that was caused by the disobedience of the devil and humankind. God's good creation was made subject to demonic powers and death, and humankind is now enslaved by selfishness, disease, alienation, and death. Through the life, death, and resurrection of Jesus Christ, believers are delivered from Satan's dominion, as well as from the effects of the Curse through the power of the Spirit. Evangelism is proclaiming God's deliverance through Jesus Christ to the entire world in the power of the Holy Spirit.

Lesson two deals with *Evangelism: The Content of the Good News of the Kingdom*. Evangelism proclaims and demonstrates God's deliverance in Christ through word as well as love and service to others. This ministry focuses on Christ; evangelism is nothing less than communicating the person and work of Jesus Christ! The Nicene Creed offers a clear useful, and powerful outline of the critical truths associated with Jesus' incarnation, passion, resurrection, ascension, and Second Coming. If we master these truths, we can clearly communicate them in our urban neighborhoods.

Our next lesson, *Evangelism: Methods to Reach the Urban Community*, reveals how evangelism is not only what we say but who we are and what we do. To speak persuasively of the Lord Jesus in our communities, our credibility must be rooted in solid character and genuine spirituality. We will look at communication methods by which to share the Good News, and the importance of preparation for effective urban evangelism through intercessory prayer. We will look at personal soul winning and sharing one's testimony, along with the importance of evangelism through public preaching and discourse. We will also consider the concept of the household network, or *oikos* in urban evangelism.

Finally in lesson four, *Follow-up and Incorporation*, we will explore the idea of conserving the fruit of our evangelism by following up new converts, that act of "incorporating new converts into the family of God so they can be equipped to grow in Christ and use their gifts for ministry." We will look at how the apostles nurtured new converts, and study how we can use the same steps to bring new converts into a local assembly of believers, on the road to spiritual maturity and fruitfulness.

Our Lord Jesus desires that we bear much fruit to the glory and praise of God (John 15.8-16). May the Lord bless your study of his Word so you can join the harvest workers in gathering the fruit of the Lord's own salvation, to the Father's glory!

- Rev. Dr. Don L. Davis

Course Requirements

Required Books and Materials

- Bible (for the purposes of this course, your Bible should be a translation [ex. NIV, NASB, RSV, KJV, NKJV, etc.], and not a paraphrase [ex. The Living Bible, The Message]).

- Each Capstone module has assigned textbooks which are read and discussed throughout the course. We encourage you to read, reflect upon, and respond to these with your professors, mentors, and fellow learners. Because of the fluid availability of the texts (e.g., books going out of print), we maintain our *official* Capstone Required Textbook list on our website. Please visit *www.tumi.org/books* to obtain the current listing of this module's texts.

- Paper and pen for taking notes and completing in-class assignments.

Suggested Readings

- Dawson, John. *Taking Our Cities for God*. Lake Mary, FL: Creation House, 1989.

- Hayford, Jack. *Answering the Call to Evangelism* (*Spirit Filled Life Kingdom Dynames Study Guides*). Nashville: Thomas Nelson Publishers, 1995.

- Phillips, Keith. *Out of Ashes*. Los Angeles: World Impact Press, 1996.

Summary of Grade Categories and Weights

Attendance & Class Participation . . . . 30%   90 pts

Quizzes . . . . 10%   30 pts

Memory Verses . . . . 15%   45 pts

Exegetical Project . . . . 15%   45 pts

Ministry Project . . . . 10%   30 pts

Readings and Homework Assignments. . . . . 10%   30 pts

Final Exam . . . . 10%   30 pts

Total: 100%   300 pts

Grade Requirements

Attendance at each class session is a course requirement. Absences will affect your grade. If an absence cannot be avoided, please let the Mentor know in advance. If you miss a class it is your responsibility to find out the assignments you missed, and to talk with the Mentor about turning in late work. Much of the learning associated with this course takes place through discussion. Therefore, your active involvement will be sought and expected in every class session.

Every class will begin with a short quiz over the basic ideas from the last lesson. The best way to prepare for the quiz is to review the Student Workbook material and class notes taken during the last lesson.

The memorized Word is a central priority for your life and ministry as a believer and leader in the Church of Jesus Christ. There are relatively few verses, but they are significant in their content. Each class session you will be expected to recite (orally or in writing) the assigned verses to your Mentor.

The Scriptures are God's potent instrument to equip the man or woman of God for every work of ministry he calls them to (2 Tim. 3.16-17). In order to complete the requirements for this course you must select a passage and do an inductive Bible study (i.e., an exegetical study) upon it. The study will have to be five pages in length (double-spaced, typed or neatly hand written) and deal with an aspect of evangelism and spiritual warfare that is covered in this course. Our desire and hope is that your participation in this course will result in an abundance of new insights into the nature of evangelism and urban ministry. As you go through the course, be open to finding an extended passage (roughly 4-9 verses) on a subject you would like to study more intensely. The details of the project are covered on pages 10-11, and will be discussed in the introductory session of this course.

Ministry Project

Our expectation is that all students will apply their learning practically in their lives and in their ministry responsibilities. The student will be responsible for developing a ministry project that combines principles learned with practical ministry. The details of this project are covered on page 12, and will be discussed in the introductory session of the course.

Class and Homework Assignments

Classwork and homework of various types may be given during class by your Mentor or be written in your Student Workbook. If you have any question about what is required by these or when they are due, please ask your Mentor.

Readings

It is important that the student read the assigned readings from the text and from the Scriptures in order to be prepared for class discussion. Please turn in the "Reading Completion Sheet" from your Student Workbook on a weekly basis. There will be an option to receive extra credit for extended readings.

Take-Home Final Exam

At the end of the course, your Mentor will give you a final exam (closed book) to be completed at home. You will be asked a question that helps you reflect on what you have learned in the course and how it affects the way you think about or practice ministry. Your Mentor will give you due dates and other information when the Final Exam is handed out.

Grading

The following grades will be given in this class at the end of the session, and placed on each student's record:

A - Superior work	D - Passing work
B - Excellent work	F - Unsatisfactory work
C - Satisfactory work	I - Incomplete

Letter grades with appropriate pluses and minuses will be given for each final grade, and grade points for your grade will be factored into your overall grade point average. Unexcused late work or failure to turn in assignments will affect your grade, so please plan ahead, and communicate conflicts with your instructor.

Exegetical Project

As a part of your participation in the Capstone *Evangelism and Spiritual Warfare* module of study, you will be required to do an exegesis (inductive study) of one of the following Scripture passages:

- ❐ 1 Corinthians 15.1-8
- ❐ Isaiah 53.3-9
- ❐ Matthew 28.18-20
- ❐ James 2.14-17
- ❐ Romans 10.8-13
- ❐ Philippians 2.19-24
- ❐ Luke 11.14-23

The purpose of this project is to give you an opportunity to do a detailed study of a major passage on the nature of evangelism, and Jesus' power to deliver from Satan and from sin and its effects. As you study one of the above texts (or a text which you and your Mentor agree upon which may not be on the list), our hope is that you will show how this text makes plain some important insight regarding evangelism, the Gospel, and sharing the Good News with others. Hopefully, too, you will be able to relate its meaning directly to your own personal walk of discipleship, as well as to the leadership role God has given to you currently in your church and ministry.

This is a Bible study project, and, in order to do *exegesis*, you must be committed to understand the meaning of the passage in its own setting. Once you know what it meant, you can then draw out principles that apply to all of us, and then relate those principles to life. A simple three step process can guide you in your personal study of the Bible passage:

1. What was *God saying to the people in the text's original situation*?

2. What principle(s) does *the text teach that is true for all people everywhere*, including today?

3. What is *the Holy Spirit asking me to do with this principle here, today*, in my life and ministry?

Once you have answered these questions in your personal study, you are then ready to write out your insights for your *paper assignment*.

Here is a *sample outline* for your paper:

1. List out what you believe is *the main theme or idea* of the text you selected.

2. *Summarize the meaning* of the passage (you may do this in two or three paragraphs, or, if you prefer, by writing a short verse-by-verse commentary on the passage).

3. *Outline one to three key principles or insights* this text provides on evangelism and spiritual warfare.

4. Tell how one, some, or all of the principles may relate to *one or more* of the following:

    a. Your personal spirituality and walk with Christ

    b. Your life and ministry in your local church

    c. Situations or challenges in your community and general society

As an aid or guide, please feel free to read the course texts and/or commentaries, and integrate insights from them into your work. Make sure that you give credit to whom credit is due if you borrow or build upon someone else's insights. Use in-the-text references, footnotes, or endnotes. Any way you choose to cite your references will be acceptable, as long as you 1) use only one way consistently throughout your paper, and 2) indicate where you are using someone else's ideas, and are giving them credit for it. (For more information, see *Documenting Your Work: A Guide to Help You Give Credit Where Credit Is Due* in the Appendix.)

Make certain that your exegetical project, when turned in meets the following standards:

- It is legibly written or typed.

- It is a study of one of the passages above.

- It is turned in on time (not late).

- It is 5 pages in length.

- It follows the outline given above, clearly laid out for the reader to follow.

- It shows how the passage relates to life and ministry today.

Do not let these instructions intimidate you; this is a Bible study project! All you need to show in this paper is that you *studied* the passage, *summarized* its meaning, *drew out* a few key principles from it, and *related* them to your own life and ministry.

Grading

The exegetical project is worth 45 points, and represents 15% of your overall grade, so make certain that you make your project an excellent and informative study of the Word.

Ministry Project

The Word of God is living and active, and penetrates to the very heart of our lives and innermost thoughts (Heb. 4.12). James the Apostle emphasizes the need to be doers of the Word of God, not hearers only, deceiving ourselves. We are exhorted to apply the Word, to obey it. Neglecting this discipline, he suggests, is analogous to a person viewing our natural face in a mirror and then forgetting who we are, and are meant to be. In every case, the doer of the Word of God will be blessed in what he or she does (James 1.22-25).

Our sincere desire is that you will apply your learning practically, correlating your learning with real experiences and needs in your personal life, and in your ministry in and through your church. Therefore, a key part of completing this module will be for you to design a ministry project to help you share some of the insights you have learned from this course with others.

There are many ways that you can fulfill this requirement of your study. You may choose to conduct a brief study of your insights with an individual, or a Sunday School class, youth or adult group or Bible study, or even at some ministry opportunity. What you must do is discuss some of the insights you have learned from class with your audience. (Of course, you may choose to share insights from your Exegetical Project in this module with them.)

Feel free to be flexible in your project. Make it creative and open-ended. At the beginning of the course, you should decide on a context in which you will share your insights, and share that with your instructor. Plan ahead and avoid the last minute rush in selecting and carrying out your project.

After you have carried out your plan, write and turn in to your Mentor a one-page summary or evaluation of your time of sharing. A sample outline of your Ministry Project summary is as follows:

1. Your name

2. The place where you shared, and the audience with whom you shared

3. A brief summary of how your time went, how you felt, and how they responded

4. What you learned from the time

The Ministry Project is worth 30 points and represents 10% of your overall grade, so make certain to share your insights with confidence and make your summary clear.

Spiritual Warfare
Binding of the Strong Man

Lesson Objectives

Welcome, in the strong name of Jesus Christ! After your reading, study, discussion, and application of the materials in this lesson, you will be able to:

- Describe carefully the truths surrounding the voluntary rebellion and disobedience of the devil and the first human pair, and how the universe as a result of this disobedience has been thrown into spiritual war.

- Show from the Scriptures that although God made the world good, because of the Fall, demonic powers were unleashed in the world, creation was made subject to corruption and death and humankind is now enslaved, subject to disease, death, alienation, and selfishness.

- Demonstrate from the Bible that salvation essentially is God's deliverance of humankind and creation through the power of the Spirit from the power and effects of sin, from Satan's dominion and tyranny and the fear of death, as well as from the effects of the Curse and sin.

- Communicate clearly how evangelism is proclaiming God's promised and prophesied deliverance through Jesus Christ to the entire world in the power of the Holy Spirit.

Devotion

Like Us to Deliver Us

Heb. 2.14-15 - Since therefore the children share in flesh and blood, he himself likewise partook of the same things, that through death he might destroy the one who has the power of death, that is, the devil, [15] and deliver all those who through fear of death were subject to lifelong slavery.

Perhaps no thought in Scripture can compare to the unusual humility of our Lord Jesus in his willingness to become like us to deliver us. This text suggests that the Lord Jesus, in his great humiliation and obedience to the Father in the Incarnation, shared in our very essence, that is, our flesh and blood in order that he might through death destroy the one who has the power of death over humankind, the devil. We will never know the depth of humility and self-forgetfulness involved in this supreme act of kindness and grace toward us. Because of the bondage that we endured due to our own sinfulness, our Lord determined to become like us, to share our weakness, to partake of the very same things we do, in order that he might break death's stranglehold on us, and liberate us for the Lord's own purpose and our new destiny. Let no one think that their own struggle or pain is unique or is in some way so extreme or rare that not even the Lord fully comprehends their hurt. This text lays to rest all thoughts that we have regarding the uniqueness of our struggle. Jesus himself became just like us in order that he might deliver us who, our whole lives long, lay under the power of sin and its inevitable result, death. Praise to the One who was willing to share in our being in order to break our very own bondage.

After reciting and/or singing the Nicene Creed (located in the Appendix), pray the following prayer:

> *O God, whose blessed Son came into the world that he might destroy the works of the devil and make us children of God and heirs of eternal life: Grant that, having this hope, we may purify ourselves as he is pure, that, when he comes again with power and great glory, we may be made like him in his eternal and glorious kingdom; where he lives and reigns with you and the Holy Spirit, one God, for ever and ever. Amen.*

~ Presbyterian Church (USA). **Book of Common Worship**. Louisville, KY: Westminister/John Knox Press, 1993. p. 236.

Nicene Creed and Prayer

No quiz this lesson

Quiz

No Scripture memorization this lesson

Scripture Memorization Review

No assignments due this lesson

Assignments Due

"Why Do Bad Things Happen to Good People?"

One evening, a little child was looking at the local news with her folks. In listening to the reports, the station told the story of a young boy who was accidentally killed by a motorist who lost control of their car on the ice, striking the young person, who died from the injuries shortly after. Later that night, filled with curiosity and questions about the incident, the little girl asked her believing mother, "Mama, you remember the story we heard about earlier, the little boy hit and killed by the car? Why did that happen? Why do things like that happen to people, even to people who haven't done anything wrong? Can't God stop things like that from happening? Why do bad things happen to good people?" How would you answer this little girl's question if you were her parent?

"There is No Devil."

In a conversation at work, during lunch hour, a mild argument broke out in the lunch room between two fellow employees. In discussing the events of 9-11, the horrific destruction of the Trade Towers in New York City, one employee claimed that this event and others like it are the work of evil people who simply are tools of the devil. The devil's lies are at the root of all evil in the world. The other employee rejected this idea, saying that evil is the result of bad choices of individuals and has nothing to do with any kind of demonic or satanic involvement. Blaming things on the devil, she said, is just an excuse for not taking personal responsibility for one's own actions. Seeming to get nowhere in their debate, they turn to you and ask your opinion. What would you say about this issue to them?

"What Can You Promise Me?"

In sharing his faith with a friend at school, a young disciple of Jesus laid out an outline of the good news of God's salvation through Jesus Christ. He explained who Jesus was, why he came to earth and had to die, and what God promises to those who receive Jesus as Lord and believe that God raised him from the dead. After listening quietly for awhile to this witness of the Gospel, the young seeker said, "That's well and good, but I am not sure if the thought of eternal life and salvation and such is all that helpful to me now. I'm broke, I lost my job two days ago, and rent is due in two weeks. I failed my midterm in English, and my girlfriend and I are struggling. I just don't see how believing in Jesus will affect my life at all. I want to go to heaven when I die, but what about today, what about right now? What can you promise me, how will my life change if I say "yes!" to Jesus today? Will it make any real difference in my life today at all?" How might the young disciple answer this question?

Spiritual Warfare: Binding of the Strong Man

Segment 1

Rev. Dr. Don L. Davis

CONTENT

1

As a result of the Fall, the universe is at war. Although God made creation good, and humankind in his own image, the rebellion of the devil and Adam and Eve has spun the world into the "Fall," resulting in the unleashing of dark demonic powers in the world, corruption and death upon creation, and slavery, suffering, and judgment upon all humankind.

Summary of Segment 1

Our objective for this first segment of *Spiritual Warfare: Binding of the Strong Man* is to enable you to see that:

- God made creation good, and humankind in his own image, with all the world and its inhabitants made good, free, and whole.

- Because of the disobedience of the devil and the first human pair, the universe has been thrown into spiritual war.

- Although God made the world good, because of the Fall, demonic powers have been unleashed upon the world, with the result being that creation has been made subject to corruption and death.

- Humankind throughout human history and the entire earth has been spiritually enslaved, subject to disease and death, and lives in alienation and selfishness.

**Video Segment 1
Outline**

I.   As a Result of the Fall, the Universe Is at War.

A. God made creation good, and humankind in his own image.

1. Ps. 24.1-2

2. Exod. 19.5

3. Deut. 10.14

4. 1 Chron. 29.11

5. Job 41.11

6. Ps. 50.12

7. The world and humankind were made good, free, and whole, with the potential for justice and love between God and all of creation.

B. The person of Satan: names given to the devil (a spirit being of unique power, enslaving the nations, opposing the Lord, causing havoc and chaos throughout human history)

1. As tempter, Matt. 4.1

2. As ancient serpent and deceiver, Rev. 12.9-10

3. As liar, John 8.44

4. As one who produces fear through death, Heb. 2.14-15

5. As wicked overlord of fallen angels, Rev. 12.4

Test Fill-in ②

C. The devil's rebellion as the operative cause of evil in the universe (pride as the source), Isa. 14.12-17   *Pride*

1. Desire to ascend to the heavens above the angels

2. Desire to make himself like the Most High

3. Certain judgment of the usurper in God's final judgment

   a. Gen. 3.15

   b. Isa. 27.1

   c. Mark 1.24

   d. Luke 10.18

   e. John 12.31

   f. John 16.11

g. Rom. 16.20

h. Col. 2.15

i. Heb. 2.14

j. Rev. 20.10

D. Adam and Eve's fall: Genesis Chapter 3

   1. *Deception*: they were deceived by the wiles of the devil.

      a. The devil's cunning lies against the first human pair, 2 Cor. 11.3

      b. The devil's ongoing work of lying and deception on us today, 2 Cor. 11.13-15

      c. Evangelism is *liberating people from the lies of the enemy*, Col. 2.8.

   2. *Disobedience*: they rebelled against the command of God.

      a. Despising God's Word, Num. 15.31

      b. Transgressing the commandment of God, 1 Sam. 15.24

c. Turning aside and refusing to obey God's voice, Dan. 9.11

d. Disobedience to God's law, Rom. 3.20

e. Transgression of the law, James 2.10-11

3. *Death*: separation from God and his life, Rom. 6.23

a. Physical suffering and death: cutting short of physical life; being made subject to disease, corruption, and death   Body die

(1) Gen. 2.16-17

(2) Gen. 3.19

(3) Rom. 5.12

b. Spiritual alienation from God and final judgment: separation from God's life and eternal judgment of the Lord   external separation of God

(1) 1 Cor. 6.9-10

(2) Gal. 6.7-8

(3) Rev. 21.8

4. The promise of salvation and deliverance: the Seed of the woman, Gen. 3.15

II. The Fallen World: General Characteristics of the Curse in a Fallen World

A. The unleashing of dark powers in the world

1. Demonic powers consigned to the earth, of the earth, Gen. 3.14

2. Demonic powers working in those who do not know the Lord, Eph. 2.1-2

3. In some sense he exercises real authority over the inhabitants of the earth, Luke 11.21-23.

4. Blinds the minds of those who do not believe, 2 Cor. 4.4

5. Is of the world, 1 John 4.4

B. The entrance of corruption and death into the world

1. Rom. 8.19-21

2. 2 Pet. 3.13

C. The fallen state of humankind: selfishness, suffering, and death

Because of the fall

④ Test
Fill-in

1. Slavery and bondage to sin

a. Prov. 5.22

b. John 8.34-36

2. Subjection to suffering and misery in all areas of life: disease and death

    a. To womankind, Gen. 3.16

    b. To Adam, Gen. 3.17-19

3. Selfishness in relationship to others: injustice

    a. Titus 3.3

    b. 2 Tim. 3.2-3

Conclusion

» God made creation good, and humankind in his own image, with all the world and its inhabitants made good, free, and whole.

» Through the disobedience of the devil and the first human pair, the universe has been thrown into spiritual war.

» Because of the Fall, demonic powers have been unleashed upon the world, with the result being that the creation has been made subject to corruption and death.

» Humankind is now spiritually enslaved, subject to disease and death, and lives in alienation and selfishness.

Segue 1

Student Questions and Response

Please take as much time as you have available to answer these and other questions that the video brought out. This segment lays out the foundational truths behind the entire subject of evangelism and spiritual war, and to understand it is critical in order to comprehend why the cross is so necessary for our redemption. Be clear and concise in your answers, and where possible, support with Scripture!

1. How does the Bible describe God's creation of the world and of humankind?

2. What are some of the names given to the person of the devil in Scripture? What does the Bible give as Satan's root motivations for his rebellion and disobedience toward God?

3. In what way does Genesis 3 describe the fall of humankind, i.e., Adam and Eve's rebellion against the Lord? How does evangelism address the deception of the devil that began in the Garden?

4. What is the difference between physical death and spiritual death?

5. The judgment of God upon the devil is certain and sure; how does Scripture describe his future judgment and destruction?

6. The "Curse" occurred as a result of the Fall. How did this event unleash spiritual powers upon the fallen universe and world?

7. How does Scripture describe the effect of the Fall upon God's created order? What judgment did God make upon the earth because of humankind's sin against him?

8. What does it mean that humankind is now subject to bondage and enslaved by sin?

9. According to the Bible, the Fall made disease and corruption a force in human life. How is this described in Genesis 3 in reference to Eve? To Adam?

10. In what way did the Fall open the door for selfishness and injustice to rule in human relationships? Explain your answer.

1

Spiritual Warfare: Binding of the Strong Man

Segment 2

Rev. Dr. Don L. Davis

Salvation is God's deliverance from the devil and liberation from the effects of the Fall, i.e., from sin and its dominion. Evangelism is the declaration of the good news of this deliverance and salvation from Satan and sin which God has accomplished for us in the person of Jesus Christ.

Our objective for this second segment of *Spiritual Warfare: Binding of the Strong Man* is to enable you to see that:

- The Bible teaches that salvation is God's deliverance of humankind and creation from the power of the devil and the effects of sin.

- Through faith in the person of Jesus Christ, those who believe can be delivered from Satan's dominion and from his tyranny (his deception and oppression) and the fear of death.

- The salvation of God in Christ also delivers those who believe from the effects of the Curse and sin through the power of the Spirit.

- Evangelism is the declaration of God's promised and prophesied deliverance through Jesus Christ to the entire world in the power of the Holy Spirit.

I.   Salvation Is Deliverance from the Power of the Devil.

   A. The purpose of the incarnation: to destroy the works of the devil

   1. Appeared to destroy the devil's works, 1 John 3.8

   2. Jesus disarmed the rulers and authorities, Col. 2.15.

3. Shared our nature to destroy the devil who had the power of death, Heb. 2.14

B. The *protoevangelium*: the first telling of the Gospel, Gen. 3.15

1. Enmity between the serpent and the woman

2. Hostility between the serpent's offspring and the woman's "Seed"

3. Bruising of the woman's offspring's heel, the crushing of the serpent's head

    a. Acts 2.23-24

    b. Rom. 16.20

    c. Eph. 4.8

    d. Rev. 12.7-8

C. The means: the life, death, and resurrection of Jesus Christ

1. His *life*: the incarnation of the glory of the Father, John 1.14-18

2. His *righteousness*: the representation of the second Adam for a new humanity, Rom. 5.17-19

3. His *death*: the penalty paid for humankind's disobedience, Rom. 5.6-9

4. His *resurrection*: the surety of God's forgiveness and grace

    a. 2 Cor. 13.4

    b. Eph. 1.19-23

II. Salvation as Deliverance from Sin and its Effects

A. Deliverance from the *penalty of sin*: Christ's substitutionary sacrifice for sin

    1. 1 Pet. 3.18

    2. Eph. 2.16-18

    3. Heb. 9.26-28

B. Deliverance from the *personage of sin*: freedom from Satan and demonic oppression

    1. 2 Cor. 2.14

    2. 1 John 4.4

3. 1 John 5.19

4. 1 Cor. 2.12

5. Eph. 6.12

Test #(1) True

C. Deliverance from the *power of sin*: the outpouring of the Holy Spirit in this age

1. Eph. 1.13-14

2. Rom. 8.14-16

3. 2 Cor. 1.22

4. Eph. 4.30

D. Deliverance from the *presence of sin*: from the in-breaking to the consummation of the Kingdom

1. 1 Thess. 5.23-24

2. 1 Cor. 1.8-9

3. Eph. 5.26-27

4.   Phil. 2.15-16

5.   1 Thess. 3.13

6.   Jude 1.24

III. Evangelism: Declaring the Good News of this Deliverance and Salvation to Those Who Need to Hear God's Message of Deliverance in Jesus Christ

A.   The *objective* side of evangelism: understanding exactly what God accomplished for creation and humankind in his work on the cross (the Good News)

1.   Apostolicity of evangelism (the apostolic tradition), 1 Cor. 15.3-8

2.   Forbidden to tamper with the Good News itself, Gal. 1.8-9

B.   The *subjective* side of evangelism: making the message of the Good News plain to every people in their own language and culture

1.   What we believe and confess, Rom. 10.8-13

2.   The necessity of a messenger, Rom. 10.14-15

Conclusion

> » Salvation is God's deliverance of humankind and creation from the power of the devil and the effects of sin.

> » Through faith in Jesus Christ, believers are delivered from Satan's dominion and deception.

> » God's deliverance in Christ also liberates believers from the effects of the Curse and sin through the power of the Spirit.

> » Evangelism is the declaration of God's promised and prophesied deliverance through Jesus Christ to the entire world in the power of the Holy Spirit.

Segue 2

Student Questions and Response

The following questions were designed to help you review the material in the second video segment. Recognizing the intimate connection between evangelism, salvation, and deliverance will greatly affect the way in which you both understand and practice biblical ministry to the lost. Be clear and concise in your answers, and where possible, support with Scripture!

1. According to the Scriptures, what precisely was the reason that Jesus came into the world? How did Jesus' death on the cross disarm the principalities and powers in their tyranny over us?

2. What is the *protoevangelium* and why is it so important for our understanding of evangelism as proclaiming the message of *God's deliverance* from satanic oppression?

3. What role does Jesus' life play in the destruction of the enemy? Be specific.

4. How did the death of Jesus accomplish for humankind its deliverance from the power of the devil, especially our fear of death and the bondage we suffer from that fear?

5. In what way does Jesus' resurrection provide us with confidence that the deliverance he won actually is accepted by God?

6. What does Scripture teach regarding Jesus' death as the sufficient penalty for our sin?

7. Why do believers never have to fear satanic domination again? What did Jesus' death and resurrection do to Satan for humankind?

8. How does the Holy Spirit guarantee us, in this age, that we are no longer under the power of sin?

9. At what point will we who believe finally be delivered from the very presence of sin?

10. Explain how evangelism is the declaration of the good news of God's deliverance from Satan and sin to those who do not believe.

CONNECTION

Summary of Key Concepts

This lesson focuses upon the foundational concepts which undergird our understanding of evangelism and spiritual warfare. Evangelism does not begin with what we do in our lives and testimonies with the lost; it began centuries ago when the devil and the first human pair rebelled against God's righteous rule. In seeking to live independent of God's authority and provision, the universe was thrown into spiritual chaos and darkness. Now, the universe is in spiritual war with God who promised to send to us a Deliverer who would crush the head of the serpent and deliver his people from their sins. Jesus Christ is that Deliverer! Understanding these basic critical points is essential in order to know just what evangelism seeks to do and what God does when those who are lost believe the good news of the Gospel.

- God made creation good, and humankind in his own image, with all the world and its inhabitants made good, free, and whole.

- Through the disobedience of the devil and the first human pair, the universe has been thrown into spiritual war, into darkness and chaos, by those disobeying God's righteous rule.

- Because of the Fall, demonic powers have been unleashed upon the world, resulting in the entire creation's subjection to corruption and death.

- Humankind is now spiritually enslaved, subject to disease and death, and lives in alienation and selfishness.

- The Bible teaches that salvation is God's deliverance of humankind and creation from the power of the devil and the effects of sin.

- Through Jesus Christ, those who believe are delivered from Satan's dominion and tyranny (his deception and oppression) and the fear of death.

- The salvation of God in Christ also delivers those who believe from the effects of the Curse and sin through the power of the Spirit.

- Evangelism is the declaration of God's promised and prophesied deliverance through Jesus Christ to the entire world in the power of the Holy Spirit.

Student Application and Implications

Now is the time for you to discuss with your fellow students your questions about the spiritual conflict which has occurred as a result of the Fall, and salvation as deliverance from the devil and sin. These concepts lie at the heart of all discussion about ministry, evangelism, and spiritual liberation. What particular questions do you have in light of the material you have just studied? Maybe some of the questions below might help you form your own, more specific and critical questions.

* Why is it important to affirm right from the beginning that the Fall, the Curse, and all the effects of sin resulted from *our rebellion* and not from *God's creation*?

* In what way is it possible for us to describe all the evil down through human history as a result of both *satanic* influence and *human* choice, refusing to live under God's righteous rule?

* In light of what we know about the bondage that creation and humankind suffer as a result of sin, why is Jesus the only one who can bring deliverance to us? Support your answer with Scripture.

* Is it fair for God to hold the entire human race accountable for the sin committed by Adam and Eve? What is the relationship of *your sinning* to *their fall*?

* How does understanding salvation as deliverance from wicked powers influence the way we think about sharing the Good News in evangelism? What should we expect when people accept the good news of salvation in Christ?

* How does the Christian *live out victoriously* the deliverance that Jesus won for them on the cross? If a believer is not living in the freedom of Christ, how might we explain what is going on in their particular situation?

Demonic Deception Versus Personal Responsibility

In counseling a family who just had a loved one run into problems with the law and the courts, the issue comes up from one family member regarding the influence of the devil in this loved one's life. She believes with all her heart that the devil's deception and influence are at the heart of what has happened to their loved one. Only demonic influence could explain his swift turn, his accepting such terrible friends, and his involvement in crime and violence. Other family members reject that view, saying that the loved one knew what was right, but decided to ignore the good teaching at home and go the route of his less-instructed friends from the neighborhood. How would you explain to this family the relationship between the devil's deception in our lives and our own personal choices to do wrong as the cause of our personal sin?

Don't Expect Change Right Away

In a meeting before a community survey/door to door campaign, a member of the elders offers a word of encouragement to the workers before they leave the church. In asking them not to be discouraged, he suggests that we ought to share the Gospel with our neighbors, praying for God's working in their lives, but that we ought not be too expectant regarding change in their lives right away. Even if they say yes to Christ, moral change requires much time and effort. Some of the workers reject this view, saying that we can expect dramatic change every time someone accepts Jesus as Lord and Savior. What is the right/best/most biblical answer for this discussion?

It's Not Our Fault

In discussing with some young men on the corner about the Good News and salvation, one of the young men rejects the idea that the neighborhood is in its tough condition because of our sin. He suggests, "For years, this country treated people who were not white as second class, not letting us vote, or work, or participate in the larger society. We didn't ask for this neighborhood, and no one in it, if they could vote on the matter, would want to live in a neighborhood where our people aren't safe, well-fed and clothed, with good jobs and nice things like everybody else. I don't care what you say! It is not our fault that things are like this. The society has never treated us right–they are the ones who have made us like this!" How would you answer this viewpoint?

Where's the Beef?

4 ▶ After studying the entire biblical idea of salvation as deliverance, one of the students in class raises an important question. "What kind of victory can we promise to people who have been living their lives for decades doing all kinds of illegal and immoral things? I have worked for years in a substance abuse program where we have shared the Lord with the participants, and many people have indicated that they have believed in Christ. Still, even after they make the profession, they continue to shoot drugs, gamble, engage in all kinds of things that I know don't please the Lord. How can we say that salvation is deliverance when so many people who claim to be saved aren't living lives full of liberation and freedom?" How would you explain these facts?

Restatement of the Lesson's Thesis

Although God created the universe good and free, it fell into darkness and chaos as a result of the disobedience of the devil and the first human pair, Adam and Eve. As a result of this Fall, demonic powers were unleashed into the universe, all of creation was placed under a Curse and made subject to bondage and corruption, and humankind was made subject to selfishness, suffering, and death. Now through the death and resurrection of Jesus Christ, God's deliverance has come to us over the devil and the effects of sin. In Jesus we have been delivered from the penalty of sin, are being delivered from the person (i.e., the devil) and the power of sin by the Holy Spirit, and soon will be delivered from the presence of sin at Jesus' Second Coming. Evangelism is declaring this deliverance through the good news of the Gospel of Christ.

Resources and Bibliographies

If you are interested in pursuing some of the ideas of *Spiritual Warfare: Binding of the Strong Man*, you might want to give these books a try:

Billheimer, Paul. *Destined for the Throne*. Minneapolis: Bethany House, 1975.

Epp, Theodore H. *The Believer's Spiritual Warfare*. Lincoln: Back to the Bible, 1973.

Hayford, Jack W. (Executive Editor). *Answering the Call to Evangelism* (*Spirit Filled Life Kingdom Dynamics Study Guides*). Nashville: Thomson Nelson Publishers, 1995.

1

Now is the time to try to isolate a principle or concept that can help you in your own particular ministry situation. Survey the various ideas, concepts, and truths that have been introduced in this lesson, and concentrate upon one insight that you will think about and pray for throughout this next week. What specific thought has the Holy Spirit impressed upon your heart regarding evangelism, spiritual warfare, and your own particular call to evangelism in your community? What particular situation or circumstance comes to mind when you think about how God has promised deliverance for those who believe the Good News? How does God want your own thinking to change in light of the truths that you have heard with your fellow students this week? Ask the Lord to give you wisdom as you pray and meditate on this lesson topic and the truth that the Spirit has impressed you with in this study.

Pray specifically that the Lord would give you his insight and understanding as you seek to understand evangelism against the backdrop of salvation as deliverance from the power of the devil and from sin and its effects. Ask God to increase your faith for results, to give you new insight into the Gospel as the very power of God unto salvation for all who believe (i.e., Romans 1.16). Ask for the Spirit's anointing as you share the Good News that the very delivering power of God might show itself in the lives of those with whom you share, even as that same power continues to transform your own life in Christ.

ASSIGNMENTS

Hebrews 2.14-15 and 2 Corinthians 11.3

To prepare for class, please visit *www.tumi.org/books* to find next week's reading assignment, or ask your mentor.

You will be quizzed on the content (the video content) of this lesson next week. Make sure that you spend time covering your notes, especially focusing on the main ideas of the lesson. Read the assigned reading, and summarize each reading with no

Ministry Connections

Counseling and Prayer

Scripture Memory

Reading Assignment

Other Assignments

more than a paragraph or two for each. In this summary please give your best understanding of what you think the main point was in each of the readings. Do not be overly concerned about giving detail; simply write out what you consider to be the main point discussed in that section of your assigned reading. Please bring these summaries to class next week. (For more information on your reading assignments, please read carefully the "Reading Completion Sheet" at the end of this lesson.)

Looking Forward to the Next Lesson

In this lesson we have seen how all creation and humankind have been made subject to bondage through the disobedience of the devil and human beings. The universe has been thrown into spiritual war because of it. The Bible declares that salvation is God's deliverance of humankind and creation from the power of the devil and the effects of sin. Through the life, death, and resurrection of Jesus Christ, believers are liberated from Satan's dominion and from the effects of the Curse and sin. Evangelism is declaring this promised and prophesied deliverance through Jesus Christ to the entire world in the power of the Holy Spirit.

In our next lesson we will look carefully at the precise content of this good news of deliverance in Jesus Christ, laying a solid biblical foundation for doing evangelism in our urban unreached neighborhoods.

1

Name _____

Date _____

For each assigned reading, write a brief summary (one or two paragraphs) of the author's main point. (For additional readings, use the back of this sheet.)

Reading 1

Title and Author: _____ Pages _____

Reading 2

Title and Author: _____ Pages _____

Evangelism
The Content of the Good News of the Kingdom

Lesson Objectives

Welcome, in the strong name of Jesus Christ! After your reading, study, discussion, and application of the materials in this lesson, you will be able to:

* Recite some of the various biblical terms in the New Testament describing the good news of the Gospel.

* Articulate how evangelism is seen as proclaiming the message of salvation in Christ as well as demonstrating that message through our love and service to others.

* Explain Romans 10.9-10 as a clear, simple, and powerful outline of the message of the Gospel.

* Show clearly how in order to win others to Jesus and train them to do the same, we simply must know the truth concerning Jesus Christ.

* Detail how evangelism is telling people of the person and work of Jesus Christ, who he is and what he did as the heart of our faith and of the Gospel.

* Highlight the main points of the Nicene Creed regarding Jesus' incarnation, passion, resurrection, ascension, and Second Coming.

* Give to others through a biblical use of the Creed a running story of the Gospel message which can be adapted as we share the message in our communities.

Devotion

Faithful to Entrust to Others the Apostolic Doctrine

1 Cor. 15.1-8 - Now I would remind you, brothers, of the gospel I preached to you, which you received, in which you stand, [2] and by which you are being saved, if you hold fast to the word I preached to you— unless you believed in vain. [3] For I delivered to you as of first importance what I also received: that Christ died for our sins in accordance with the Scriptures, [4] that he was buried, that he was raised on the third day in accordance with the Scriptures, [5] and that he appeared to Cephas, then to the twelve. [6] Then he appeared to more than five hundred brothers at one time, most of whom are still alive, though some have fallen asleep. [7] Then he appeared to James, then to all the apostles. [8] Last of all, as to one untimely born, he appeared also to me.

The Apostle Paul gave to others in his evangelistic ministry the precise story and doctrine which had been passed down to him. This message, this deposit, was the instrument of the Lord which, if believed, resulted in the salvation of the believer's soul. The very core of that message was the person and work of Jesus Christ, the Messiah of God who died for our sins according to the Scriptures, was buried, and rose again according to the same scriptural testimony. The message states that this risen Lord Jesus then appeared to a number of witnesses, and lastly to him. This simple, elegant, and straightforward message is the good news of deliverance, the word of truth that liberates everyone who believes. The heart of evangelism is the faithful entrustment of this good news to reliable people who can teach others also (2 Tim. 2.2). Nothing is more critical for the messenger of God than faithfully passing on what the apostles have given to us. We pass on the apostolic word with neither change nor amendment. We are stewards of the mysteries of God (1 Cor. 4.1-2), and it is critical that we be found faithful. We must receive it, guard it, love it, and tell it boldly to others. Those who tell the Gospel best are those who have been changed most by its message. Are you committed to guard the deposit which the apostles gave to us, the Good News of Christ?

After reciting and/or singing the Nicene Creed (located in the Appendix), pray the following prayer:

Nicene Creed and Prayer

> *Almighty and Ever-living God, in your tender love for the human race you sent your Son our Savior Jesus Christ to take upon him our nature, and to suffer death upon the cross, giving us the example of his great humility: Mercifully grant that we may walk in the way of his suffering, and also share in his resurrection; through Jesus Christ our Lord, who lives and reigns with you and the Holy Spirit, one God, for ever and ever. Amen.*

~ The Episcopal Church. **The Book of Common Prayer and Administrations of the Sacraments and Other Rites and Ceremonies of the Church, Together with the Psalter or Psalms of David** New York: The Church Hymnal Corporation, 1979. p. 219.

Quiz

Put away your notes, gather up your thoughts and reflections, and take the quiz for Lesson 1, *Spiritual Warfare: Binding of the Strong Man.*

Scripture Memorization Review

Review with a partner, write out and/or recite the text for last class session's assigned memory verses: Hebrews 2.14-15 and 2 Corinthians 11.3.

Assignments Due

Turn in your summary of the reading assignment for last week, that is, your brief response and explanation of the main points that the authors were seeking to make in the assigned reading (Reading Completion Sheet).

Gospel of the Kingdom or Gospel of the Grace of God

 Jehovah's Witnesses had been canvassing the neighborhood, and when they dropped by your apartment last week they asserted that the only gospel which Jesus preached was the Gospel of the Kingdom, which is in fact different from the Gospel of the Grace of God which the Christian churches normally speak about in their meetings. The Gospel of the Kingdom is the *rule of God's sovereignty* made available for all who join Jehovah's organization, the Jehovah's Witnesses. All other gospel presentations, according to those who were canvassing, is not from Jehovah but man-made. What is the relationship between the two (if in fact they are two) gospels, i.e., the Gospel of the Kingdom and the Gospel of the Grace of God?

More Showing, Less Telling

In discussing the need for Gospel preaching with a Christian relief representative, the person made a statement that demanded a response. She said, "The problem with so many of you Bible-believing types is that you love to preach at others but you refuse to just love people where they are. I believe that you can preach the Good News by not even saying a single word. You guys would do yourselves much good if you did more showing of the Gospel with deeds of compassion and less telling of it with words." What do you think about her statement?

2

3

Actions, Not Doctrines, Is What Is Important in Ministry

Two students in discussing the importance of the truth in Gospel ministry disagreed strongly on the role of doctrine in evangelism. While one student thought doctrine to be the very core of the message and therefore of evangelistic ministry, the other felt that discussions about unproven and unprovable theological doctrines only muddies the waters for seekers interested in learning about Jesus. Too much discussion of doctrine can actually interfere with the presentation of the Good News, it was claimed. What is the role of doctrine in sharing the Good News with the lost? As far as doctrine is concerned, should we load up or travel light?

Evangelism: The Content of the Good News of the Kingdom

CONTENT

Segment 1: Biblical Content of the Gospel

Rev. Dr. Don L. Davis

Summary of Segment 1

The one true Gospel of God in Jesus Christ is known by a number of different names, all of which point to the good news of God's grace offered to us through faith in Christ Jesus. Evangelism is proclaiming the person and work of Jesus Christ and God's offer of redemption in him, as well as confirming that message through a practical display of love and service to the needy and the broken. Romans 10.9-10 provides us with a clear and effective outline of the essential elements of the content of the Good News in Christ.

Our objective for this segment, *Biblical Content of the Gospel*, is to enable you to see that:

- The Gospel (i.e., Good News) of Christ is known by a number of names in the New Testament, all of which point to God's offer of redemption and deliverance in the person of Jesus Christ.

- Evangelism is seen in Scripture both (and primarily as) proclaiming the message of salvation in Christ and demonstrating that message through our love and service to others.

- Romans 10.9-10 provides a clear, simple, and powerful understanding of the message of the Gospel as confession of Jesus' lordship and faith in his resurrection from the dead.

Video Segment 1
Outline

I. Biblical Terms for the Good News

A. *Evangelion*: good tidings

    1.   Two senses in the New Testament: active proclamation of the message and the content being proclaimed

    2.   1 Cor. 9.14, "In the same way, the Lord commanded that those who proclaim the Gospel [i.e., *the content of the Gospel*] should get their living by the Gospel [i.e., *proclamation of the Gospel*])."

    3.   The objective content of the Good News

        a.   The message regarding Christ, 1 Cor. 15.3-5

        b.   The heart of apostolic preaching, 2 Tim. 2.8-9

        c.   The power of God for salvation, Rom. 1.16-17

    4.   Response to the Gospel - the critical element in salvation, 2 Thess. 1.6-8

B. Names given to the Good News in the New Testament

    1.   The Gospel of God

        a.   Mark 1.14

2

   b. Rom. 1.16-17

   c. 1 Thess. 2.9

 2. The Gospel of his Son, Rom. 1.9

 3. The Gospel of Jesus Christ, the Son of God, Mark 1.1

 4. The Gospel of our Lord Jesus, 2 Thess. 1.8

 5. The Gospel of the Glory of Christ, 2 Cor. 4.4

 6. The Gospel of the Grace of God, Acts 20.24

 7. The Gospel of the Glory of the Blessed God, 1 Tim. 1.11

 8. The Gospel of your Salvation, Eph. 1.13

 9. The Gospel of the Kingdom

   a. Matt. 4.23

   b. Matt. 9.35

   c. Matt. 24.14

C. General observations

1. The Gospel is central to the Church's identity and ministry.

2. The Gospel focuses on the person and work of Jesus Christ.

3. The Gospel is the very power of God for deliverance and salvation to those who hear it and receive it.

II. Evangelism as Both Demonstration and Proclamation of the Good News

A. Evangelism as "telling by showing;" demonstrating the Good News

1. Through our good works

   a. Created by God for good works, Eph. 2.8-10

   b. Through our good works those who see them glorify God, Matt. 5.14-16

2. Through our unity and love in the Church, John 17.20-23

3. Through our obedience and allegiance to the Lord, Titus 2.11-14

B. Evangelism as "telling as well as showing": communicating the Good News

1. In public preaching

a. With clarity about Jesus Christ

(1) Repentance toward God and faith in Jesus Christ, Acts 20.20-24

(2) Preaching Jesus Christ and him crucified, 1 Cor. 2.1-5

b. Open testimony before the minds and consciences of others

(1) Before God in Christ, 2 Cor. 2.17

(2) Simply, with godly sincerity, 2 Cor. 1.12

(3) Open statement of the Gospel, 2 Cor. 4.2

2. In private testimony

a. Philip and the eunuch, Acts 8.35-36

b. Always ready at all times, public and private, 2 Tim. 4.1-2

Evangelism

Test

3. Accompanied by much labor and suffering

a. Sharing in suffering for the Gospel, 2 Tim. 1.8-9

b. Becoming a fool for Christ's sake, 1 Cor. 4.10-13

c. Paul's record of commitment, 2 Cor. 11.23-27

d. Filling up what is lacking in Christ's afflictions, Col. 1.24

e. Enduring suffering in ministry, 2 Tim. 4.5

III. The Gospel Outline: the Key Facts of Romans 10.9-10

Rom. 10.9-10 - because, if you confess with your mouth that Jesus is Lord and believe in your heart that God raised him from the dead, you will be saved. [10] For with the heart one believes and is justified, and with the mouth one confesses and is saved.

A. Clause one: if you confess with your mouth: the lordship of Christ

1. Confession with the mouth as sign of both conviction and allegiance

2. The content of confession: the absolute sovereignty of Jesus Christ over all

   a. Jesus died and rose to be Lord, Rom. 14.7-9.

   b. All shall one day confess Jesus as Lord, Phil. 2.9-11.

B. Clause two: if you believe in your heart: the death, burial, and resurrection of Christ for sin

1. Christ Jesus actually physically died.

a.   Jesus crucified and killed, Acts 2.22-23

      b.   Killing of the Author of Life, Acts 3.13-15

  2.   His body was buried in a tomb where it lay lifeless for three days.

      a.   Made his grave with the wicked, Isa. 53.9

      b.   The historical accounts of the Gospels agree on his burial, Matt. 27.57-60.

  3.   The third day God raised Jesus from the dead.

      a.   Presented himself alive with proofs, Acts 1.3

      b.   Christ's judgship confirmed by the resurrection, Acts 17.31

      c.   If Christ is not raised, Christian faith is futile, 1 Cor. 15.16-21.

      d.   God brought Jesus back from the dead, Heb. 13.20.

C. Clause three: if you confess Jesus as Lord and believe in his saving work on the cross, *you shall be saved*.

  1.   Confession of Jesus' lordship is made unto salvation.

2.   Belief in Jesus' death and resurrection is made unto righteousness.

Conclusion

»   The Gospel (i.e., Good News) of Christ is known by a number of names in the New Testament, all of which point to God's offer of redemption and deliverance in the person of Jesus Christ.

»   Evangelism is seen in Scripture both (and primarily as) proclaiming the message of salvation in Christ and demonstrating that message through our love and service to others.

»   Romans 10.9-10 provides a clear, simple, and powerful understanding of the message of the Gospel as confession of Jesus' lordship and faith in his resurrection from the dead.

Segue 1

Student Questions and Response

Please take as much time as you have available to answer these and other questions brought out in the video teaching segment. Understanding the essential content of the Gospel is the first and perhaps most significant step in sharing the Good News effectively with those who have neither heard nor understood God's offer of redemption in Jesus. Be clear and concise in your answers, and where possible, support with Scripture!

1.   List three of the various names given to the good news of salvation in Jesus Christ by the authors of the New Testament. In what way is the Gospel central to the Church's very identity and ministry?

2.   What is the significance of the Gospel's focus upon the person and work of Jesus Christ?

3.   What is the role of the demonstration of works of love and service to the Gospel? Is such demonstration necessary to give a complete understanding of the Good News itself? Why or why not?

4.   In what way does the unity of the Church actually enable people to know that our Gospel offer in Christ is legitimate and trustworthy?

5.   In what ways does the existence of a submitted, obedient community of believers actually aid in the proclamation of the Gospel message to others?

6. What elements must we be absolutely clear on when we share the good news of God's salvation in Jesus Christ? What role does the message of the cross play in Gospel presentation?

7. According to Jesus and the apostles, what is the relationship of labor and suffering to the actual presentation of the Gospel message to others?

8. In Romans 10.9-10, what is the relationship between confession and belief? What precisely must the believer *confess* and *believe* in order to be saved (delivered) by God?

9. Can one be saved and forgiven if they deny the physical resurrection of Jesus Christ? Why or why not?

10. What is the sure promise in Romans 10.10 for the one who confesses Jesus as Lord, and believes in their heart that God raised him from the dead?

2

Evangelism: The Content of the Good News of the Kingdom

Segment 2: Nicene Creed Content

Rev. Dr. Don L. Davis

Authentic evangelism is Christo-centric, in other words, it is centered on the person and work of Jesus of Nazareth and the claims made about his death, burial, and resurrection from the grave. To grasp the essential doctrine of Christ Jesus is essential for all God-honoring evangelism, and the Nicene Creed provides a biblically informed, historically accepted testimony of who Jesus is and what his entrance into the world produced.

Our objective for this segment, *Nicene Creed Content*, is to enable you to see that:

- In order to win others to Jesus and train those already won to do the same, we simply must know the truth concerning Jesus Christ. Evangelism is telling people of the person and work of Jesus Christ!

- A thorough knowledge of who Jesus is and what he did lies at the heart of our faith and of the Gospel.

Summary of Segment 2

- The doctrinal content of the Good News message is contained in the Nicene Creed, which provides a clear, useful, and powerful outline of the critical truths associated with Jesus' incarnation, passion, resurrection, ascension, and Second Coming.

- A mastery of the content of the Creed will provide us with a running story of the Gospel message which can be adapted as we share the message in our communities.

The Nicene Creed (325 A.D.)

We believe in one God, the Father Almighty, Maker of heaven and earth and of all things visible and invisible.

We believe in one Lord Jesus Christ, the only Begotten Son of God, begotten of the Father before all ages, God from God, Light from Light, True God from True God, begotten not created, of the same essence as the Father, through whom all things were made.

Who for us men and for our salvation came down from heaven and was incarnate by the Holy Spirit and the virgin Mary and became human. Who for us too, was crucified under Pontius Pilate, suffered and was buried. The third day he rose again according to the Scriptures, ascended into heaven, and is seated at the right hand of the Father. He will come again in glory to judge the living and the dead, and his Kingdom will have no end.

We believe in the Holy Spirit, the Lord and life-giver, who proceeds from the Father and the Son, who together with the Father and Son is worshiped and glorified. Who spoke by the prophets.

We believe in one holy, catholic, and apostolic Church.

We acknowledge one baptism for the forgiveness of sin, and we look for the resurrection of the dead and the life of the age to come. Amen.

2

I. Jesus Came Down from Heaven and Became Human.

A. Pre-existent Christ: Jesus is the Word which was with God from the beginning.

1. Mic. 5.2

2. John 8.58

3. John 1.1-2

B. The Word became flesh.

1. 1 John 1.1-3

2. John 1.14

3. John 1.18

4. Implications

a. Jesus was the Son of God in his pre-existent state.

b. Jesus became a human being through the power of the Holy Spirit, born of the Virgin Mary.

    c. As a human being and God, he was a perfect mediator between humankind and the Lord.

      (1) 1 Tim. 2.5-6

      (2) Heb. 7.25

      (3) Heb. 8.6

      (4) Heb. 12.24

II. He Was Crucified, Suffered, and Was Buried: He Died on the Cross.

A. Jesus was crucified under a Roman official's tenure: crucified under Pontius Pilate, John 19.16-19.

    1. An actual historical figure

    2. At a particular time in human history

B. Jesus suffered physically and died on the cross: the suffering of Jesus Christ.

    1. Jesus' suffering was real, 1 Pet. 2.21-24.

    2. Jesus' suffering was vicarious (done in our place as a substitution for us), Isa. 53.3-6.

C. Jesus' dead body was laid in a tomb: the burial of Jesus Christ, Matt. 27.58ff.

2

III. The Third Day He Arose from the Dead: the Resurrection of Christ.

A. The third day according to the Scriptures

1. Ps. 2.7

2. Ps. 16.10-11

3. Isa. 53.10-12

4. Matt. 12.40

5. Acts 2.25-28

B. The meaning of the resurrection for evangelism

1. As sign of God's acceptance of Jesus' sacrifice, Rom. 5.9-10

2. As display of the total victory, Col. 2.13-15

3. As first-fruits of God's saving work for humankind, 1 Cor. 15.20-23

4. As justification of Jesus' deity and identity, Rom. 1.1-4

IV. He Ascended and Is Seated at God's Right Hand: the Ascension and Session of Christ.

A. Ascended to the Father's right hand: Jesus as exalted Prince and Savior

   1. All authority is given to the risen Jesus, Matt. 28.18-20.

   2. Jesus leads evangelistic efforts from his exalted place with the Father, Acts 2.32-36.

B. Session in heaven: Jesus as reigning Lord of all

   1. Jesus is the Glorified Son of God, God's Regent, Heb. 1.1-4.

   2. Jesus is the Head of the Church, Eph. 1.20-23.

   3. Jesus is the Lord of the harvest, (the Giver of the Great Commission).

      a. He will be with us always in our mission, to the end, Matt. 29.19-20.

      b. He is Lord of the harvest, Matt. 9.35-38.

V. He Will Come Again to Consummate His Kingdom: the Coming Reign of Jesus Christ.

A. He will come again to judge the living and the dead.

1. All judgment is given to Jesus, John 5.21-23.

2. Jesus will be the judge of the living and the dead.

   a. Acts 10.42

   b. 2 Tim. 4.1

3. God will judge the world in righteousness in Jesus, Acts 17.31.

2

4. All must appear before the judgment seat of Christ, 2 Cor. 5.10.

B. His Kingdom will have no end.

1. Evangelism is rooted in the prophetic promise of God's eternal Kingdom in Christ, Ps. 89.35-37.

2. Jesus is the Son of Man who will reign forever, Dan. 7.13-14.

3. Gabriel's message to Mary will come about: his reign over his people will have no end, Luke 1.30-33.

Conclusion

» In order to win others to Jesus and train those already won to do the same, we simply must know the truth concerning Jesus Christ. Evangelism is proclaiming boldly to others the person and work of Jesus Christ!

» A thorough knowledge of who Jesus is and what he did lies at the heart of our faith and of the Gospel.

» The doctrinal content of the Good News message is contained in the Nicene Creed, which provides a clear, useful, and powerful outline of the critical truths associated with Jesus' incarnation, passion, resurrection, ascension, and Second Coming.

» A mastery of the content of the Creed will provide us with a running story of the Gospel message which can be adapted as we share the message in our communities.

Segue 2

Student Questions and Response

The following questions were designed to help you review the material in the second video segment. The Nicene Creed provides us with a clear, useful, and concise outline of the doctrinal content of the Good News message, focusing as it does on his incarnation, passion, resurrection, ascension, and Second Coming. Rehearse these details clearly and concisely, supporting your views always where possible with Scripture!

1. What does the Creed assert about Jesus' person before he came down from heaven and became human, i.e., who was he before he took on human form?

2. In what way did the Holy Spirit and the Virgin Mary combine their activities to produce the human being, Jesus of Nazareth?

3. Why is it necessary in the content of the Gospel to assert that Jesus was actually physically crucified, that is, that he actually died on the cross?

4. What does it mean when we say that Jesus' suffering for humankind was "vicarious?" What does the burial of Jesus signify regarding his death and departure from this world?

5. List three Old Testament Scriptures which refer to the resurrection of Messiah as a prophecy.

6. What is the meaning of the resurrection of Messiah Jesus in regards to our salvation, and therefore, our evangelism?

7. How does the ascension relate to our understanding of Jesus as Lord of all today? Describe Jesus' present session in heaven–what is he doing at the present time at the Father's right hand?

8. The Creed asserts that Jesus will return at the End of the Age to accomplish certain tasks. What are they, and what is their relationship to evangelistic ministry?

9. What is the relationship between proclaiming salvation through the good news of Christ and the need for Jesus to have risen from the dead, as the Old Testament Scriptures prophesy?

10. Explain the sentence: "Evangelism is rooted in the prophetic promise of God's eternal Kingdom in Christ," Ps. 89.35-37.

2

Summary of Key Concepts

This lesson focuses upon the importance of solid biblical doctrinal content in all evangelistic ministry. Evangelism that is effective finds its alpha and omega in the person and work of Jesus Christ, who himself is its central message and focus. In order to equip others for evangelism, and to be equipped ourselves, we must master the Word of God regarding the person of Jesus, giving those who hear it a full and clear understanding of God's working in Christ to save us and liberate us to be his people under his reign.

- While the Gospel (i.e., Good News) of Christ is known by a number of names in the New Testament, all of them refer to the same message, i.e., God's offer of redemption and deliverance in the person of Jesus Christ.

- Evangelism is seen in Scripture both (and primarily as) *proclaiming the message of salvation* in Christ and *demonstrating that message through our love* and service to others.

- Romans 10.9-10 provides a clear, simple, and powerful understanding of the message of the Gospel as *confession of Jesus' lordship* and *faith in his resurrection* from the dead.

- In order to win others to Jesus and train those already won to do the same, we simply must *know the truth concerning Jesus Christ*. Evangelism is telling people of the person and work of Jesus Christ!

- A thorough knowledge of *who Jesus is and what he did* lies at the heart of our faith and of the Gospel.

- The doctrinal content of *the Good News message is contained in the Nicene Creed*, which provides a clear, useful, and powerful outline of the critical truths associated with Jesus' incarnation, passion, resurrection, ascension, and Second Coming.

☞ A mastery of the content of the Creed will provide us with a running story of the Gospel message which can be adapted as we share the message in our communities.

Student Application and Implications

Now is the time for you to discuss with your fellow students your questions about the content of the good news of the Gospel. The Gospel must be proclaimed and demonstrated, and the essence of the Good News is the confession of Jesus' lordship and faith in God's raising him from the dead. A clear, expanded doctrinal content of the Good News message is contained in the Nicene Creed, which provides a useful and powerful outline of the critical truths associated with Jesus' incarnation, passion, resurrection, ascension, and Second Coming. To understand this outline, you must train yourself to answer your own particular questions of the material you have just studied. Maybe some of the questions below might help you form your own, more specific and critical questions.

* In what way can we know for certain that the various titles and names given to the Gospel in the New Testament actually refer to the one and the same Gospel? (See Gal. 1.8-9)

* Is it fair to suggest that the demonstration of the Gospel is as important as the actual telling of the Good News itself? Defend your answer with Scripture.

* What is the meaning of the phrases in Romans 10: "confessing with your mouth that Jesus is Lord and believing in your heart that God raised him from the dead?" Are these merely intellectual professions or something else? How can you know you have confessed and believed credibly?

* Why is affirming that Jesus actually physically died and rose so important to the Gospel, and therefore so central for the evangelistic message?

* What role does faith in Jesus' resurrection from the dead play in the Gospel message? Can one be saved and not believe that Jesus *physically* rose from the grave? Why or why not?

* How much of Jesus' person and work should an evangelist know in order to make the message most plain to those who have never heard of God's offer in Christ?

Character, Not Content

In a recent evangelistic youth rally, a youth minister spent very little time covering any of the doctrinal content of the Gospel with the kids participating in the event. He reasoned, "Doctrine only creates unnecessary discussions about stuff that doesn't matter. I figured I would rather have a handful of kids on fire for the Lord and in love with him than a bunch of folks hung up on big theological words and weird ideas about the resurrection and incarnation and other doctrinal issues." Do you agree or disagree with the rationale of the youth minister? Why or why not?

That Kind of Thing Doesn't Help Anybody

Concerned that their food outreach ministry was becoming too silent about the Good News, a Christian worker brought up in a ministry meeting the need for the team to share the Gospel more openly and clearly. One of the fellow workers objected to the proposal, saying "We speak most clearly of the love of God in Christ with these folks when we show our care for them in our food ministry, clothing distribution, our crisis counseling, and overall care for them. When we make the focus of the time on preaching at them, we inevitably cast a shadow on our love and service, and they become objects rather than fellow human beings who need our love. If you ask me, preaching is overrated. The ones who usually preach the loudest serve the least. Frankly, that kind of thing doesn't help anybody." How would you respond?

Makes No Sense to Me

In sharing with a seeker who is close to accepting the Lord, you notice more and more of the ideas of the Jehovah's Witnesses in his speech. You grow very concerned when he asserts calmly and logically that Jesus' body never rose from the dead, only his spirit was resurrected by God. He shows you in his JW textbook how this is the case, which quotes 1 Corinthians 15.45 - Thus it is written, "The first man Adam became a living being"; the last Adam became a life-giving spirit. He demands strongly from you an answer to his question: *Why do I need to believe that Jesus rose from the dead physically in order to be saved? That simply makes no sense to me.* How would you answer his question?

Too Heavy of a Load to Bear

 In an evangelistic training session at church, a young Christian is disappointed and discouraged. She enrolled in the course because she was interested in sharing the Lord with a number of her coworkers, and thought the course would be a wonderful blessing to help her prepare for this. Once in the course, however, she was stunned at how much the instructor suggested they needed to know in order to share the simple message of the Good News with others. She had shared Christ with others before, but never knew any of this "new stuff" the instructor was talking about. Frustrated, she asks you why do you have to know all of that doctrinal stuff if all you want to do is to share Jesus' love with others. When is enough enough already? How much do we need to know in order to share the Lord effectively with others?

Restatement of the Lesson's Thesis

Although the New Testament provides a number of titles to the good news of Grace in Christ, they all refer to the one, true offer of God's grace in Jesus. The Gospel must be proclaimed in word and demonstrated in love, and the essence of the Good News is the confession of Jesus' lordship and heart faith in God's raising him from the dead. A clear, expanded doctrinal content of the Good News message is contained in the Nicene Creed, which provides a clear, useful, and powerful outline of the critical truths associated with Jesus' incarnation, passion, resurrection, ascension, and Second Coming.

Resources and Bibliographies

If you are interested in pursuing some of the ideas of *Evangelism: The Content of the Good News of the Kingdom* you might want to give these books a try:

Ladd, George Eldon. *The Gospel of the Kingdom*. Grand Rapids: Eerdmans, 1999.

Shenk, David W. And Ervin R. Stutzman. *Creating Communities of the Kingdom*. Scottsdale, PA: Herald Press, 1998.

Snyder, Howard A. *Kingdom, Church, and World*. Eugene, OR: Wipf and Stock Publishers, 1985.

Ministry Connections

The idea of the Gospel and its content is critical to your ministry, and undoubtedly the Holy Spirit has highlighted a particular issue or idea for you that has a real practical ministry connection unique to your own life and ministry. Survey your

2

own thoughts and insights at this point, and observe what the Lord might be suggesting to you about your own focus or application of these insights in your work today. What, in particular, is the Holy Spirit suggesting to you in regards to your own mastery of the content of Good News, especially your ability to defend and display the person of Christ in your sharing with others? What particular situation comes to mind when you think about how the Lord may want you to make even clearer the truth as it is in Christ? Ask the Lord to clarify your own specific areas of connection on these and other related points.

Do not hesitate to do additional study in this area with your mentor or others, as the Lord leads. Perhaps you need to rehearse these truths to become better acquainted with the Scriptures on these subjects, or the Lord is asking you to meditate on these and other texts to get a better grasp of the content of the Good News. Ask the Holy Spirit to direct you as you continue to equip yourself in your ability both to share and to prepare others to share the Good News of Christ.

Counseling and Prayer

ASSIGNMENTS

Romans 10.9-10

Scripture Memory

To prepare for class, please visit *www.tumi.org/books* to find next week's reading assignment, or ask your mentor.

Reading Assignment

Make certain to set aside plenty of time for your memorization work, and do not forget to read carefully the assignments above, and as last week, write a brief summary for them and bring these summaries to class next week (please see the "Reading Completion Sheet" at the end of this lesson). Also, now is the time to begin to think about the character of your ministry project, as well as decide what passage of Scripture you will select for your exegetical project. These assignments will be upon you quickly, *so do not delay* in determining either of them. The sooner you identify your interests and select your topics, the more time you will have to prepare!

Other Assignments

Looking Forward to the Next Lesson

We have now covered some of the essential foundational issues regarding evangelism and spiritual warfare. We understand its theological roots in the Fall and the Curse, and the new hope we receive through understanding evangelism as the declaration of God's deliverance through Christ. Evangelism is both the proclamation of the message of salvation in Christ and its demonstration in love and service to others. We have also seen how the Nicene Creed reveals the Christ-centered nature of the Christian Gospel.

In our next lesson, we will turn our attention to understand the ways in which our very lives, words, and deeds can reach men and women in our unreached, urban neighborhoods.

2

Name _____

Date _____

For each assigned reading, write a brief summary (one or two paragraphs) of the author's main point. (For additional readings, use the back of this sheet.)

Reading 1

Title and Author: _____ Pages _____

Reading 2

Title and Author: _____ Pages _____

LESSON 3

Evangelism
Methods to Reach the Urban Community

Lesson Objectives

Welcome, in the strong name of Jesus Christ! After your reading, study, discussion, and application of the materials in this lesson, you will be able to:

- Share with others the kind of lifestyle and conduct we as leaders must adopt in order to touch our urban communities.

- Show from Scripture how evangelism is not only what we say but who we are and what we do (i.e., evangelism must be rooted in solid character and genuine spirituality).

- Recite what kind and quality of spirituality we need to have to be a credible witness to God's grace in Christ (through our walk with God, our relationship with our families, and with outsiders).

- Demonstrate with Scripture the importance of a lived faith, of being zealous to do good works, especially on behalf of those who are poor and most vulnerable.

- See how we can prepare for effective evangelism through prevailing intercessory prayer.

- State from the Bible the importance of the roles of personal soul-winning, public preaching, and discourse in evangelism.

- Give an overview of the importance of the concept of the household network or *oikos* in urban evangelism.

3

Devotion

Evangelism, Jesus Style

Matt. 25.41-46 - Then he will say to those on his left, "Depart from me, you cursed, into the eternal fire prepared for the devil and his angels. [42] For I was hungry and you gave me no food, I was thirsty and you gave me no drink, [43] I was a stranger and you did not welcome me, naked and you did not clothe me, sick and in prison and you did not visit me." [44] Then they also will answer, saying, "Lord, when did we see you hungry or thirsty or a stranger or naked or sick or in prison, and did not minister to you?" [45] Then he will answer them, saying, "Truly, I say to you, as you did not do it to one of the least of these, you did not do it to me." [46] And these will go away into eternal punishment, but the righteous into eternal life.

Jesus' teaching about the judgment in Matthew 25 represents one of the most important yet troubling discourses our Lord ever gave us about the nature of salvation and of true intimacy with him. It is fashionable in many settings today to attribute salvation to the one who bows their head at the end of the hymn of invitation in an evangelistic meeting, or to the person who raises their hand at the preacher's request at the invitation at the conclusion of a revival service. Jesus describes real relationship with him in an entirely different way. Those who know him, those who inherit eternal life and the Kingdom which God has prepared for his own, are those whose lives demonstrate extraordinary mercy towards the hungry, the thirsty, the stranger, the naked, the sick, and the imprisoned. Those who know Christ inadvertently pour out their service and grace upon these broken and battered, and realize at the judgment, to their utter amazement, that they have actually been ministering instead to the Lord himself. Jesus, in this text, completely redefines the religious life; it is not merely understanding facts and being able to communicate data; pure religion is about the concrete demonstration of compassion to the broken and despised, whose identification with Messiah is so complete that to care for them is to care for him. What would happen if we completely redefined the doctrine of "assurance of salvation" to mean caring for the hungry, the thirsty, the stranger, the naked, the sick, and the imprisoned. This would be to capture salvation and evangelism in a new way, to do it, *Jesus style*. May God give us the grace to see through the eyes of the Lord and to see those who really are in fact the very *Christ in another person*.

After reciting and/or singing the Nicene Creed (located in the Appendix), pray the following prayer:

> *Keep, O Lord, your household the Church in your steadfast faith and love, that through your grace we may proclaim your truth with boldness, and minister your justice with compassion; for the sake of our Savior Jesus Christ, who lives and reigns with you and the Holy Spirit, one God, now and for ever. Amen.*

~ The Episcopal Church. **The Book of Common Prayer and Administrations of the Sacraments and Other Rites and Ceremonies of the Church, Together with the Psalter or Psalms of David.** New York: The Church Hymnal Corporation, 1979. p. 230

Nicene Creed and Prayer

Quiz	Put away your notes, gather up your thoughts and reflections, and take the quiz for Lesson 2, *Evangelism: the Content of the Good News of the Kingdom*.

....

Scripture Memorization Review	Review with a partner, write out and/or recite the text for last class session's assigned memory verse: Romans 10.9-10.

....

Assignments Due	Turn in your summary of the reading assignment for last week, that is, your brief response and explanation of the main points that the authors were seeking to make in the assigned reading (Reading Completion Sheet).

....

Credentials

 In a recent outreach at church, Mother Williams, one of the oldest and most refreshing Christians in our entire fellowship showed up on a Saturday to attend our door to door canvassing campaign in our church. This canvassing demanded that those involved attend at least four of the six training meetings meant to prepare our workers for the kinds of responses they would encounter during their sharing the Gospel with our neighbors. Mother Williams, who desperately wanted to attend the meetings, was only able to make three of the six training sessions. She is arguably the most spiritual, most biblical, and most refreshing Christian in the church, with a long and wonderful record of teaching, training, and sharing her faith everywhere, naturally. Should Mother Williams be allowed to canvass today–why or why not?

A Little Too Fresh

Recently, our church welcomed a minister, an intern, who will be working with the church for the next year in its outreach and mission efforts. As a graduate from a fine evangelical seminary, the intern is well trained in Scripture and the biblical languages, is experienced in ministry from an associates position at another church, and has served several times on short terms missions outreaches both overseas and in other urban communities. The intern is perfect for the position, except he simply doesn't show respect for others. In all that he says and does he communicates a "holier-than-thou" attitude to the other members of the team, and demonstrates an attitude of superiority to the members of the outreach committee. He is well liked by the congregation in general, and the pastor considers the church lucky to have him for a year. What should the committee members do to challenge the young, fresh intern with a superior attitude?

Ignorant and Unlearned

Without a doubt, the finest evangelist in our church is a person who can barely read and yet loves the Lord. Everyone knows that this sister has the gift of evangelism; she can share from virtually any text of the Bible, turn it to an evangelistic message, and make an appeal to others that leads them to repent and believe in Christ. A fine Christian, a wonderful mother, with a strong burden for ministry, she has been talking to the pastor about the possibility of taking on some role at the church in equipping others to share their faith. The pastor is excited about the possibility, but knows that other members will be concerned that she is neither academically skilled nor trained, although she is the most gifted evangelist he has ever seen. What advice would you have for the pastor if he asked you if he should pursue this sister as a member of his staff to equip others for evangelistic outreach?

Evangelism: Methods to Reach the Urban Community

Segment 1: Our Walk with God

Rev. Dr. Don L. Davis

To evangelize is to live a life that displays the beauty of the Lord, involving the kind of character and maturity that communicates the power of the Gospel alongside our words and presentations. Our walk with God must precede our speaking for God.

Our objective for this segment, *Our Walk with God*, is to enable you to see that:

- Our lifestyle and conduct must coincide with our language and testimonies as we share the Good News in urban communities.

- Evangelism is not only what we say but who we are and what we do. The credibility we need to speak persuasively of the Lord Jesus in our communities must be rooted in solid character and genuine spirituality.

Summary of Segment 1

- To evangelize is to live a life that displays the beauty of the Lord, i.e., becoming a certain kind of person whose life communicates the power of the Gospel alongside our words and presentations.

- We prove our faithfulness in witness by our relationship with God, our families, and with outsiders.

- The credible testimony which serves as a solid foundation for Christian witness is a lived faith, reflected in a zeal to do good works, especially on behalf of those who are poor and most vulnerable.

Video Segment 1 Outline

I. We Are Solidly Converted to Jesus Christ as Disciples: Personal Experience of God's Forgiveness through Faith in Jesus Christ.

 A. Personal repentance and faith in Jesus Christ

1. Paul's exhortations to the Corinthians: examine yourselves, 2 Cor. 13.5-6.

 2. Evangelism is based on personal preparation.

   a. Ps. 17.3

   b. Ps. 26.2

   c. Ps. 119.59

   d. Ps. 139.23-24

3

3. We exhort others to follow Christ even as we ourselves are following him, 1 Cor. 11.1.

4. We discipline ourselves lest we be cast away even after telling others about Christ, 1 Cor. 9.24-27.

5. We cultivate a strong walk with Christ as a challenge to others to follow our own example, Phil. 3.13-17.

B. Ability and desire to communicate one's personal faith in Christ

1. Rom. 15.14

2. We must be strong enough to teach others the Word of God, Heb. 5.12-14.

   a. However young a Christian might be, they must know the Word well enough to explain what God has done in their lives and why.

   b. We must be committed to doing our part in sharing the Gospel so that the Great Commission might be fulfilled through us.

3. If we know the Word of God, we must ask God for an open heart that is ready and willing to share the Good News with others.

   a. 2 Tim. 2.2

   b. 1 Pet. 3.15

4. Without question, the most effective method of urban evangelism is the ongoing display of a transformed life, Matt. 5.14-16.

II. Consistent Display of Christlike Character in the Family, the Body of Christ, and before Outsiders

A. Loving relationships within the family

1. As a son or daughter, Eph. 6.1-3

2. As a spouse, 1 Pet. 3.7

3. As a parent

a. As spiritual leaders in the home, Josh. 24.15

b. As keepers of the faith for future generations, Deut. 4.9

c. As instructors in the way of the Lord, Eph. 6.4

4. As kinfolk within a clan

a. 1 Tim. 5.4

b. 1 Tim. 5.8

B. In good fellowship in one's Christian community

1. Member in good standing in a local church, Gal. 6.2

2. Investment of time and money in the well-being of the members of the body, John 13.34-35

3. Edifying relationship with leaders and pastors, Heb. 13.17

Test

C. Credible and compelling testimony before outsiders

1. On the job

   a. As a boss

      (1) Just and fair treatment, Col. 4.1

      (2) Without threats and intimidation, Eph. 6.9

      (3) Fair wages, Lev. 19.13

      (4) Oppression of workers will undermine your ministry, Isa. 58.3

      (5) God is mindful of unjust practices, James 5.4

   b. As an employee

      (1) Sincere legitimate work as to Christ, Eph. 6.5-8

      (2) Not merely with eye-service, Col. 3.22

2. In your neighborhood and larger community, 1 Pet. 3.8-12

3. In your contacts with outsiders

a. Col. 4.5-6

b. Ps. 90.12

c. Matt. 10.16

d. 1 Pet. 3.15-16

III. A Zeal for Good Works: Justice and Mercy on Behalf of the Poor

A. Why is a zeal for good works so critical for credible urban evangelism?

Test

1. Treatment of the poor as barometer of spiritual vitality, Isa. 58.5-12

2. A faith that is alive, James 2.14-17

3. As evidence of the indwelling love of God, 1 John 3.16-18

4. As token of the display of religion in its purest form, James 1.27

5. As sign of ministering vicariously to the Lord Jesus himself, Matt. 25.41-46

3

B. Adopt a lifestyle that ministers love, service, and justice for the poor

1. Go to where they live, work and play and serve them there, John 12.24-26

2. Be discreet, Matt. 6.2-4

3. Be generous to those who are needy, 2 Cor. 9.6-8

4. Serve those who cannot return the favor

    a. Luke 14.12-14

    b. Luke 6.32-36

5. Share from your own goods, 1 John 3.16-18

6. Show no favoritism to those rich and powerful, James 2.5-6

Evangelism must be a way of life, a kind of living in the world where our conduct and relationships communicate our allegiance to Jesus and pave the way for us to share the Good News with others.

"Share the Good News with the lost, and if necessary, use words!"

~ St. Francis

Conclusion

» Evangelism is not merely talking and presenting, it is displaying and showing.

» Evangelism begins with our own quality of life and testimony, our walk before God, our family, our neighbors, and our community.

Segue 1

Student Questions and Response

Please take as much time as you have available to answer these and other questions on the relationship of evangelism to one's own character and credibility. Be clear and concise in your answers, and where possible, support with Scripture!

1. Why is it necessary for someone to be a follower of Christ *before* they become an effective *evangelist for Christ*?

2. How is providing a personal example to others an integral part of the actual evangelistic task? How does the lifestyle of the *evangelist* reflect either positively or negatively upon the meaning of the Gospel itself?

3. Why can't one's ministry ever exceed the bounds of their own depth and maturity in Christ? Is this so . . . can we share *more* than we actually *are* in our personal lives? Explain your answer.

4. Why is the display of a transformed life so critical for urban evangelism and outreach?

5. What should our response be to those who desire to minister in Christ's name but whose family relationships are fractured and broken? Are there limits in this, and if so, what are they?

6. Why does the New Testament place such importance on the need for a compelling testimony in one's life for those who represent the good news of the Kingdom?

7. The Bible places great emphasis on maintaining a credible testimony with those who are outsiders as we bear witness to Christ. Why should we seek to maintain an honorable reputation before those who don't even know the Lord–why is that important to evangelism?

8. Is a zeal for good works, especially among the poor and despised, an important element in evangelism in the city? Why or why not?

3

9. What steps ought we to take regarding someone who is in a formal role of sharing the Good News and yet their personal lives are out of order? Explain.

10. Complete the following sentence. "Those who would have a powerful evangelistic ministry in the city, must prepare themselves for the work by _____."

Evangelism: Methods to Reach the Urban Community

Segment 2: By Word of Mouth

Rev. Dr. Don L. Davis

3

We prepare for effective evangelism first and foremost through a structured program of prevailing intercessory prayer. Urban evangelism involves personal soul-winning as well as public preaching and evangelistic outreach. The most effective form of urban evangelism is along the lines of family and friendship networks, or the biblical concept of the household network or *oikos*.

Summary of Segment 2

Our objective for this segment, *By Word of Mouth*, is to enable you to see that:

- The foundation and ground of all effective urban evangelism is a programmed, consistent ministry of prevailing intercessory prayer.

- In order to reach as many of our neighbors as possible, we must encourage the practice of personal soul-winning and sharing one's testimony, as well as public preaching and evangelistic outreach.

- The most effective principle of penetrating urban communities with the Gospel is through the biblical concept of the household network or *oikos*. Helping individual believers share the Gospel in the context of their *oikia* lies at the heart of all equipping in urban evangelism.

Household

I. Urban Evangelism Demands and Should Be Preceded by Continuing and Prevailing Intercessory Prayer.

A. Why is prayer important to evangelism?

1. People are spiritually blinded to the truth of the Gospel.

2. People are enslaved under the authority and domination of the devil, Matt. 12.25-30.

3. Prayer is a mighty weapon in spiritual ministry, associated with categorical promises of the Lord.

a. John 14.13

b. John 15.16

c. John 16.23

d. 1 John 5.14

4. Prayer has the ability to tear down strongholds and fortresses, opening people's hearts and minds up to the Lord.

a. 2 Cor. 10.3-5

b. Matt. 26.41

3

c.   Luke 21.36

d.   Col. 4.2

e.   1 Pet. 4.7

5.   God alone draws men and women, boys and girls to himself.

a.   John 12.32

b.   John 6.44

c.   John 6.39-40

d.   Rom. 9.16-18

6.   Certain kinds of bondages are extraordinarily difficult to overcome.

a.   Mark 9.29

b.   James 5.15

B.   What kind of prayer should accompany our evangelistic efforts?

1.   Faithful and consistent, 1 Thess. 5.16-18

2. Specific and targeted, Eph. 6.18-20

3. Fervent and strong, Rom. 12.12

4. Expectant and full of conviction, Heb. 11.6

C. Many methods of prayer are available for effective urban evangelism.

1. Concerts of prayer

2. Prayer walks

3. Prayer vigils

4. Special convocations of prayer

II. **Urban Evangelism Is Built upon Training Urban Disciples to Personally Win Souls and Share Their Testimony with Others.**

A. Why is personal evangelism so important?

1. It is the way most people come to the Lord.

2. We are always to be ready to share our faith, 1 Pet. 3.15.

3

a. Ps. 119.46

b. Luke 21.14-15

3. The redeemed of the Lord should say so.

a. Ps. 107.2

b. Acts 5.29

B. The New Testament provides numerous examples of personal testimony.

1. Jesus and the Samaritan woman, John 4.1-42

2. Paul the Apostle before Agrippa, Acts 26

3. Philip and the Ethiopian Eunuch, Acts 16.24-34

4. Andrew with his brother Simon, John 1.41-45

5. Peter and John before the Sanhedrin, Acts 4

C. Rule of thumb: sharing one's personal testimony should be seen as simply rehearsing our life journey which led us to faith in Christ for someone, and what has happened since we believed in him.

1. Critical Examples

    a. Paul's testimony before Agrippa, Acts 26

    b. Paul's history in Galatians, Gal. 1-2

2. Characteristics of Paul's testimony

    a. Personal

    b. Clear

    c. Concise

    d. Appealing

D. Implications and suggestions for developing your personal testimony

    1. Be biblical.

    2. Be personal.

    3. Be clear.

    4. Be brief.

5. Be real.

6. Be patient.

III. Urban Evangelism Takes Place When Unbelievers Are Exposed to the Gospel through Public Preaching and Discourse.

A. Why is public evangelism so important?

1. The example of public evangelism is dominant in the Scriptures (e.g., Acts chapters 2, 4, 6, 10 etc.).

2. Millions have responded to Jesus Christ through evangelism in public places: time-tested effectiveness.

3. Public evangelism can take advantage of those who have the gift of evangelism.

   a. Eph. 4.11

   b. 2 Tim. 4.5

4. Members of the assembly can invite their friends and family to come and hear the Good News.

5. We can go to where the people are and share with them in context (the emphasis on "going").

a. Matt. 28.19-20

b. Mark 16.15-16

c. Acts 1.8

B. The gift of evangelism: every member evangelism versus the work of the evangelist

1. Every Christian should share their faith, but God has given some the gift of evangelism.

2. No model is effective which ignores the importance of gifted evangelists in the Church.

3. No approach is valid that discourages ordinary believers from sharing their own personal testimony with the lost.

C. Principles to remember in public evangelism

1. The Good News emphasizes God's work in history, 1 Cor. 15.1-4.

2. God has chosen the foolishness of preaching to make the Good News known to the lost, 1 Cor. 1.17-18.

3. The message must be contextualized to fit the audience, 1 Cor. 9.19-22.

4. Spiritual antagonism exists in every presentation, 2 Cor. 4.3-4.

5. The Holy Spirit must empower the messengers while simultaneously bringing light to the heart and mind of the hearers.

    a. 1 Cor. 2.14

    b. 1 John 2.27

    c. 1 John 5.20

6. The spiritual readiness of the hearer determines their response, not reliance on methods or techniques, Matthew 13.

D. Practical advice for public evangelism

1. Recruit intercessors to lay the proper prayer foundation.

2. Be free and innovative, but remain sensitive to the receiving culture.

3. Be organized; make certain all mechanics for the event and meeting are well planned and outfitted.

4. In all preaching, boldly declare and focus on Christ.

5. Enlist spiritual laborers to gather up the harvest.

6. Make the Gospel appeal clear.

7. Be prepared for seekers and responders.

8. Keep careful records (for following up decisions and interest).

IV. Through Penetration of the *Oikos*

The Gospel was spread according to our New Testament narratives and accounts through people who shared the Gospel naturally in the context of the households that they lived in (cf. Mark 5.19; Luke 19.9; John 4.54; 1.14-15; etc.). Cornelius is a prime example of how the Gospel spread through the shared life and connection that families and friends had in the Roman **oikos.**

A. The dimensions of the *oikos* (circle, web, networks)

1. Common *kinship relationships* (immediate, extended, and adopted family members)

2. Common *acquaintances and friendships* (friends, neighbors, those sharing common experiences, interests, loyalties)

3. Common *associates* (work and business relationships, special interests, recreation, ethnic or cultural affinities, national or political allegiances)

B. Why *oikos* evangelism is critical for urban ministry

1. It is biblical. Jesus and the apostles ministered in this way; the Gospel spread naturally through relational networks (historically fruitful approach).

A household usually contained four generations, including men, married women, unmarried daughters, slaves of both sexes, person without citizenship, and "sojourners," or resident foreign workers.
~ Hans Wolff.
Anthology of the Old Testament.

3

a. Andrew and his brothers, John 1.40-42

b. The Philippian Jailer, Acts 16.30-33

c. Cornelius, Acts 10.24

2. Most natural and least threatening means to share the Good News among a people (no cold calling, all lifestyle and friendship evangelism)

3. Receptivity of *oikos* members to others within their circle (builds on the shared history, commitments, backgrounds, and concerns of the members)

4. Credibility gap of being an "outsider" becomes irrelevant for *oikos* members

5. Expands and clarifies traditional missions language about "people group" or "target population" to other unique people groupings

6. Allows for rapid penetration of a group with the Gospel, faster than any other way

7. Makes follow-up of new Christians less awkward, strained, or impersonal

8. Allows entire family groups to be targeted

9. Gives the Holy Spirit opportunity to take advantage of any relationship within the *oikos* as the entry point of greater ministry

C. Implications of the *oikos* for urban evangelism

1. Think of the entire network, not just individuals when you minister in neighborhoods or projects.

2. Start with the relationships and contacts God provides.

3. When targeting new groups, do your demographic work.

4. Enlist the help of new believers immediately as "apostles" to their *oikos* (e.g., Andrew to Peter [John 1], the Samaritan woman to her hometown, [John 4]).

5. Look for ways to extend relationships deeper into the *oikos*.

6. Train faithful believers to share their faith within their own webs and circles; pray for the Spirit's empowerment for them, Acts 16.

Conclusion

» Urban evangelism involves establishing programs of consistent, prevailing intercessory prayer, both for those who share and for those who hear the Good News.

» Effective evangelistic outreach will equip individual Christians to win souls by sharing their personal testimony.

» Public preaching and evangelistic outreach must be a critical element in all urban evangelism and ministry to the lost.

» Entire networks of friends and kinship relationships can be penetrated through a focused, prayerful outreach to the various household networks, or the individual *oikos* of each Christian in their own sphere of influence.

The following questions have been created to help you review the material in the second video segment. The emphasis was on sharing the Good News verbally, with a focus especially on the need for prayer, for private and public evangelism with special attention being given to the individual webs of influence or *oikos* of those to whom we share the Good News. Be clear and concise in your answers, and where possible, support with Scripture!

Segue 2

Student Questions and Response

1. Why is prayer such a critical element in all effective urban evangelism? What are the characteristics of the kind of prayer that sets the foundation for meaningful outreach in the city?

2. What are some of the specific ways in which we can organize ourselves as we prepare for urban evangelism through structured, focused intercessory prayer?

3. Being able to share one's testimony is critical for urban evangelism. What elements are involved in the activity of personal soul-winning?

4. List two instances in the New Testament where an evangelistic witness is done personally to one person or a small private group. What do we learn about personal soul winning from these examples?

5. What is the *rule of thumb* for sharing your personal testimony, and how do you best prepare to be able to share your personal testimony of faith with others?

6. What elements must be included in a clear, biblical, and personal testimony of one's faith in Christ?

7. Write out your testimony. Can you give your personal testimony of faith with Scripture in 3 minutes or less? Write out a version that allows you to do this.

8. Why is public evangelism so important for sharing the Good News? Give at least four biblical reasons.

9. What is the difference between having the *gift* of evangelism and *doing the work* of an evangelist? Why should we ask God to provide us with those who possess the *gift of evangelism* and well as provide all of us with a *zeal to evangelize*?

10. What is an *oikos*, and why is this concept so important for urban evangelism?

11. How should the idea of *oikos* influence our planning and programming as we seek to win our urban communities with the Gospel of Christ?

CONNECTION

Summary of Key Concepts

This lesson focuses upon both the kind of character and methods of communication that are most effective in sharing the Good News in urban communities. An evangelistic program or outreach that is staffed by credible disciples of Jesus who can share their own testimonies both privately and publicly with power and clarity is the kind that will see great results before the Lord. In the end, all fruit comes from the Lord (1 Cor. 3.7 - So neither he who plants nor he who waters is anything, but only God who gives the growth.) The best we can do is to become the kinds of vessels whom the Holy Spirit can use when and where he wills to proclaim the good news of God's deliverance in our neighborhoods. Some of the critical ideas for this lesson include:

☞ *Our lifestyle and conduct must match up with and back up our language and testimonies* as we share the Good News in urban communities.

☞ Evangelism is not only *what we say* but *who we are* and *what we do*. The credibility we need to speak persuasively of the Lord Jesus in our communities must be rooted in solid character and genuine spirituality.

☞ To evangelize is to *live a life that displays the beauty of the Lord*, i.e., becoming a certain kind of person whose life communicates the power of the Gospel alongside our words and presentations.

☞ *We prove our faithfulness in witness by our relationship* with God, with our family, and with outsiders.

3

↦ The credible testimony which serves as a solid foundation for Christian witness is *a lived faith, reflected in a zeal to do good works*, especially on behalf of those who are poor and most vulnerable.

↦ Urban evangelism involves establishing programs of *consistent, prevailing intercessory praye*r, both for those who share and those who hear the Good News.

↦ Effective evangelistic outreach will *equip individual Christians to win souls* by sharing their personal testimony.

↦ *Public preaching and evangelistic outreach* must be a critical element in all urban evangelism and ministry to the lost.

↦ *Entire networks of friends and kinship relationships* can be penetrated through a focused, prayerful outreach to the various household networks, or the individual *oikos* of each Christian in their own sphere of influence.

Now is the time for you to discuss with your fellow students your questions about discovering credible ways to communicate the Good News in our urban communities. Hopefully you have seen that evangelism can never be reduced down to techniques and methods; *evangelism*, in the end, is about the calling and preparation of *evangelists*, those set apart to represent the Lord and his kingdom message. Surely as you have considered these ideas, the Lord, the Holy Spirit, has spoken to you about some aspect of your own life and ministry that he wants you to address. As you have covered these texts of Scripture, what particular questions have arisen about your own life and ministry? Maybe some of the questions below might help you form your own, more specific and critical questions.

Student Application and Implications

* What kind of testimony do I currently have right now, in my family, among the believers in my fellowship, and with those who are on the outside?

* Are there areas in my own personal life that currently disqualify me from representing the Lord? What is the Spirit saying to me about those areas?

* Am I equipped adequately to share my personal testimony one on one or in a private setting with others? How do I get prepared to share my testimony, using Scripture and my own personal journey with the Lord?

3

*   Do I show any signs of having the *gift of evangelism*? Who can I ask who might be able to confirm my questions about my evangelistic gifts–my believing family members, my small group, my pastor, others?

*   What is my own sense of penetrating my particular *oikos* with the Gospel? Who are the members of my immediate and extended family, my friends, and my associates whom I can begin to pray for an opportunity to share the Good News with?

*   As one charged with equipping others for ministry, what are the ways I can help prepare those under my charge with the skills and attitudes to share the Good News within their own *oikos* networks? What is the first step to preparing them for greater impact in the Gospel?

CASE STUDIES

Winning the Older Ones through the Younger Ones

1 The vision of the children's ministry in church is simple: present the Gospel to every child in our church and the surrounding neighborhood. Knowing that each of the children is part of a larger *oikos* of kinships, friendships, and associate relationships, how might we challenge the children's ministry to expand their outreach to become a *springboard* into a pool of new relationships, rather than a *backstop* of only focusing on the children themselves?

First Things First

2 A young person who possesses one of the most likeable personalities and most popular reputations among the unsaved high schoolers of her school recently became a Christian. Because she is so popular, such an able communicator, and is completely willing to take the lead in youth ministry outreach, she seems like a natural to put in charge of the youth ministry's upcoming high school outreach. She is a very new Christian, however, who is a little unclear about the nature of the Christian faith and walk, and still struggling with some of the "loose ends" of her previous life. There is a lively discussion about whether or not to use her as the "front man" for the outreach; if she were, attendance would go up greatly (because she is so popular at school). Others feel it is simply too soon to place her up front before she has a chance to grow up some in Christ. What would you advise the outreach team to do with her?

3

Those Who Have Ears to Hear

A gentle struggle has begun to develop between two distinct groups in church. One group is convinced that the historic practice of the church for the last 25 years of being blunt and hard hitting with the Gospel from the pulpit is the only responsible way to share the faith. Others, who have been persuaded by the "seeker sensitivity" models of outreach, are suggesting that we can attract more people first through our works of love and charity, and then explain the details of the Gospel once the people know that we care for them. The pastor can see the problem brewing, but is at a loss to determine which "style" his church should adopt. How might he approach the issue to solve this challenge between the two groups in his church?

Evangelism is not only what we *say* but who we *are* and what we *do* (i.e., evangelism must be rooted in solid character and genuine spirituality). We prove to be faithful stewards of God's Gospel when we back up our witness with a credible walk with God, loving relationship with our families, and solid reputations with outsiders. This stewardship is known by the demonstration of a zeal for good works, especially on behalf of those who are poor and most vulnerable. Such an effective evangelist prepares by prevailing intercessory prayer, personal soul-winning and public preaching, and focuses on the concept of the household network or *oikos* in urban evangelism.

Restatement of the Lesson's Thesis

If you are interested in pursuing some of the ideas of *Evangelism: Methods to Reach the Urban Community*, you might want to give these books a try:

Resources and Bibliographies

Arn, Win and Charles Arn. *The Master's Plan for Making Disciples.* 2nd Ed. Grand Rapids: Baker Book House, 1998.

Snyder, Howard A. *Community of the King.* Downers Grove: InterVarsity Press, 1977.

------. *Liberating the Church: The Ecology of Church and Kingdom.* Downers Grove: InterVarsity Press, 1983.

Ministry Connections

Thinking about the truth of Scripture through its interconnection with your own life and ministry is the key to making the Word of God come alive in your personal life. Meditate upon the central teachings of this lesson, and ask the Lord how he might want you to change or alter your ministry approach based on these truths. The Holy Spirit is a Person of freedom and creativity (2 Cor. 3.17), and if you listen carefully to him in this regard he will direct you to apply the Word of God in new ways within your own personal life situation. His voice is living and personal; he may be directing you to apply these truths in new ways in your own ministry situation right now. Set aside some time this week to be in his presence and listen to him as he directs you to apply this teaching on evangelistic method, and promptly respond to his leading as he directs. Of course, anything he reveals this week, be ready to share those prompting and insights with the other learners in your class.

Counseling and Prayer

As the Holy Spirit surfaces particular issues through your study and discussion of this material, turn his insights and promptings into prayer for yourself and others. Find a partner in prayer who can share your burdens with you, and together lift up your requests to God. Of course, your Mentor is open to hearing your insights and desires, and your church leaders, especially your pastor, may be specially equipped to help you answer any difficult questions arising from your reflection on this study. Be open to God and allow him to lead you as he determines.

3

▶ **ASSIGNMENTS**

Scripture Memory

2 Timothy 2.24-26

Reading Assignment

To prepare for class, please visit *www.tumi.org/books* to find next week's reading assignment, or ask your mentor.

Other Assignments

Now is the time for you to be prepared for your other assignments. As usual you ought to come with your reading assignment sheet for this week's reading material. *Also, you must have selected the text for your exegetical project, and turn in your proposal for your ministry project. Do not be tardy on your selections; you will delay your work and shorten your time to concentrate on these important assignments.*

We have completed our third lesson of this module, focusing upon the idea that evangelism begins with our own quality of life and testimony, our walk before God, our family, our neighbors, and our community. We have also seen how prevailing intercessory prayer, personal and public evangelism, and concentration on household networks or *oikos* can make a difference as we seek to share the Good News of Christ in our neighborhoods.

In our last and final lesson, we will concentrate on *following up and incorporating new believers in our fellowships*, i.e., how giving new converts special nurture and care can conserve the fruit of our evangelism, and establish these new brothers and sisters as they journey toward spiritual maturity in Christ.

Looking Forward to the Next Lesson

3

Name _____

Date _____

For each assigned reading, write a brief summary (one or two paragraphs) of the author's main point. (For additional readings, use the back of this sheet.)

Reading 1

Title and Author: _____ Pages _____

Reading 2

Title and Author: _____ Pages _____

LESSON
4

Follow-Up and Incorporation

Lesson Objectives

Welcome, in the strong name of Jesus Christ! After your reading, study, discussion, and application of the materials in this lesson, you will be able to:

- Defend the idea that the key to successful evangelism is following up new Christians by incorporating them into a local assembly of believers as quickly as possible.

- Provide a biblical definition of follow-up and incorporation of new believers in the Church as "incorporating new converts into the family of God so they can be equipped to grow in Christ and use their gifts for ministry."

- Recite the reasons for follow-up: follow-up of new believers is critical because new Christians are vulnerable to attack from the enemy, they need to be reoriented to their new faith in Christ, and they need immediate parental care as little newborns in Christ.

- Give the five biblical methods of apostolic follow-up: prevailing prayer, immediate personal contact with the new believers, sending representatives for encouragement and challenge, regular personal correspondence, and appointing leaders over them.

- Lay out the biblical rationale for baptism and membership with a local body as a means of publicly testifying of their new-found faith.

Devotion

Raising Your Children in the Lord

1 Thess. 2.7-12 - But we were gentle among you, like a nursing mother taking care of her own children. [8] So, being affectionately desirous of you, we were ready to share with you not only the gospel of God but also our own selves, because you had become very dear to us. [9] For you remember, brothers, our labor and toil: we worked night and day, that we might not be a burden to any of you, while we proclaimed to you the gospel of God. [10] You are witnesses, and God also, how holy and righteous and blameless was our conduct toward you believers. [11] For you know how, like a father with his children, [12] we exhorted each one of you and encouraged you and charged you to walk in a manner worthy of God, who calls you into his own kingdom and glory.

4

The Bible is a book of analogies and metaphors, all of which "image forth" the truth and provide us with meaning through concrete pictures. One of the more graphic pictures of ministry is viewing those whom we lead to the Lord as our spiritual children, our offspring, our newborns. Placing new believers in this analogy provides us with loads of concrete insight into the nature of ministry. If evangelism is conception and birth, then follow-up and incorporation is raising your children in the Lord. It would be entirely irresponsible to go around and, for the sheer pleasure of sexual intercourse and fruitful abundance, have as many children as we could with no thought of parenting the offspring that was conceived. While it only requires genetics to be a father, it takes commitment and love to become a daddy, and patience and perseverance to become a grandpa. Paul envisioned himself as a parent, a papa, a daddy who was raising his children in the Lord, feeding them, disciplining them, strengthening them, and nurturing them. His kindly exhortation and encouragement to the young Thessalonian believers was like a father exhorting and encouraging his own children. What a wonderful picture of the kind of affection, care, and protection our evangelism should lead to. Evangelism without nurture is loving the pleasure of conception and running away from the responsibility of delivery, infancy, childhood, and child rearing. No system of evangelism is good that ignores the obvious responsibility to raise your spiritual children in the Lord. If you enjoy birth, you are responsible for growth. There is no way around it.

4

After reciting and/or singing the Nicene Creed (located in the Appendix), pray the following prayer:

> *Faithful God, you formed your Church from the despised of the earth and showed them mercy, that they might proclaim your salvation to all. Strengthen those whom you choose today, that they may faithfully endure all trials by which you conform your Church to the cross of Christ.*

> ~ Presbyterian Church (USA). **Book of Common Worship**. Louisville, KY: Westminister/John Knox Press, 1993. p. 103.

Nicene Creed and Prayer

Quiz

Put away your notes, gather up your thoughts and reflections, and take the quiz for Lesson 3, *Evangelism: Methods to Reach the Urban Community.*

Scripture Memorization Review

Review with a partner, write out and/or recite the text for last class session's assigned memory verse: 2 Timothy 2.24-26.

Assignments Due

Turn in your summary of the reading assignment for last week, that is, your brief response and explanation of the main points that the authors were seeking to make in the assigned reading (Reading Completion Sheet).

On a Super Roll

1 ▶ As you visit a neighboring prison in your region and share the Lord with the inmates, you see a brother with a remarkable gift of sharing the Lord, leading many individuals to the Lord through the Gospel. Yet, this dear brother seems to have no sense whatever of the need to follow up or incorporate these new converts into a body of believers. When others mentioned this omission to him, he seemed to have had little or no concern about the fate of these newborns in Christ, and suggested that his gift is to ensure their presence in the Kingdom as an *evangelist*, and others with different gifts are to ensure their growth and strength. What, if anything, is wrong with this brother's conception of evangelism that it includes no forethought of the health of his spiritual offspring?

"I'll Do That Later."

2 ▶ A dear brother has recently come to the Lord after many months of prayer and sharing the Scriptures with him. A person of a fairly notorious background filled with distrust and animosity, the Lord warmed his heart to the Lord sometime last month, and he has been hungry for the Lord ever since. He refuses, however, to come to church and fellowship with other Christians. He views his new found faith as a personal private decision, his own individual religion that has little or nothing to do with what others think and do. He says he has had some bad experiences at church before, and he is not anxious now to be baptized or hang out with "those folks." He suggests, "Meeting with you like this is great, but I don't know about

4

being with those people. Not right now . . . I'll do that later." How should we respond to his opinion of church and fellowship, baptism and membership?

"Them People Is All Crooks."

Just recently a family accepted Christ at a church picnic. On a follow-up visit with them, the Wilsons told you that they like to come to church and are very excited about growing in Christ. Yet, a bad previous experience that the husband had with a pastor has made him dramatically skeptical of the motives of any clergyman. He views them all as crooks, in it for the pride, the money, and the glory (among other things). Mr. Wilson's view surfaced again when he was going through a Membership Class. This week's lesson was on "Our Need for Pastoral Care" and you talked about the need for new and growing Christians to be under godly pastoral oversight. For the first time since their decision, the Wilsons appear nervous and doubtful, and are struggling with the idea of submission to pastoral leadership being important for their personal faith. How would you approach the Wilsons to help them understand the need for ongoing pastoral care as growing believers?

4

Follow-Up and Incorporation

Segment 1: Personal Follow-Up of Individual Believers

Rev. Dr. Don L. Davis

CONTENT

Evangelism and spiritual warfare that results in the conversion of new believers in Christ requires a solid and responsible program of follow-up, incorporating the new converts into a healthy, growing assembly of disciples through baptism and full membership in the body.

Summary of Segment 1

Our objective for this segment, *Personal Follow-Up of Individual Believers*, is to enable you to see that:

 The key to successful evangelism is following up new Christians by quickly incorporating them into a local assembly of believers.

- To follow up new believers in Christ consists of "incorporating new converts into the family of God so they can be equipped to grow in Christ and use their gifts for ministry." This is for the purpose of maturity and fruitfulness.

- New believers must be followed up quickly because they are vulnerable to attack from the enemy, they need to be reoriented to their new faith in Christ, and they need immediate parental care as little newborns in Christ.

- The New Testament provides five ways that the apostles followed up new converts in Christ, all of which we can still do today. We can prevail for them in intercessory prayer, provide immediate personal contact, send personal representatives for encouragement and challenge, maintain regular personal correspondence, and ensure that they have solid spiritual leaders over them.

Video Segment 1
Outline

I. What Is the Meaning of the Concept "Follow-Up?"

Definition: "Follow-up is incorporating new converts into the family of God so they can be equipped to grow in Christ and use their gifts for ministry."

A. "Incorporating new converts into the family of God"

1. New believers must be welcomed into the family of God, Rom. 15.5-7.

2. Evangelism's goal is fellowship: with God in Christ and with the other members of the body of Christ, 1 John 1.1-3.

B. "So they can be equipped to grow in Christ"

1. The Great Commission is to make disciples, not converts, Matt. 28.19-20.

2. Christian growth occurs in the context of body life, not just individual activities, Rom. 12.4-6.

3. Christlikeness is the explicit aim of union with Christ.

    a. Rom. 13.14

    b. 1 Cor. 15.49

    c. 2 Cor. 3.18

    d. Eph. 4.24

    e. 1 John 3.2

4. *Edification* is the first major goal of follow-up: new Christians are called to live the Christian life in community so they can grow up to maturity in Christ.

    a. 1 Cor. 8.1

    b. 1 Cor. 14.12

    c. Eph. 4.29

    d. 1 Thess. 5.11

C. "And use their gifts for ministry and service"

    1. Every Christian is given special gifts to be used in ministry, 1 Cor. 12.4-7.

    2. Every member of the body of Christ has a role to play for the upbuilding of the body, 1 Pet. 4.10-11.

    3. God wants every Christian to be fruitful and to contribute to the fulfillment of the Great Commandment and Great Commission *in the context of a local assembly of believers.*

        a. The Great Commandment: new Christians bear fruit as they learn to love God with all their heart, mind, soul, and strength, and their neighbor as themselves, Matt. 22.37-40 (cf. the new commandment of John 13.34-35).

        b. The Great Commission: new Christians bear fruit as they learn to use their gifts to make disciples of Jesus Christ, Matt. 28.19-20.

    4. *Fruitfulness* is the second major goal of follow-up: new Christians were created unto good works, loving service and bold witness of the Gospel.

        a. John 15.16

        b. John 15.8

        c. Rom. 1.13

4

d. 1 Cor. 3.6-7

II. Why Is Follow-Up Necessary When Evangelism Occurs?

A. New converts are vulnerable to attack from the enemy and need protection, Acts 20.28-31.

    1. Note the parable of the sower, Matt. 13

        a. The devil's direct interference

        b. The persistent cares of this world

        c. The shallow rootedness of new believers in their faith

        d. Proneness to error and deception

    2. Paul was very concerned about the establishment of new believers in the faith.

        a. The Thessalonians, 1 Thess. 3.1-5

        b. The Galatians, Gal. 3.1-4

        c. The Philippians, Phil. 1.23-26

4

B. New converts need to be reoriented to their new identity in Christ with the family of God as soon as possible.

1. The need for placement in the body; no member can function as an isolated unit, 1 Cor. 12.14-20.

2. New believers need to be re-oriented to the will and life of God: basic doctrinal instruction, Heb. 5.11-14.

3. Need to cultivate a new, strong sense of belonging to the family of God, 1 John 3.1-2

4. Critical concern for ongoing protection and security in the flock (predators prey on the young and the sick), 1 Pet. 5.8-9

5. New Christians need to be introduced to their Christian sisters and brothers, forming new and lasting friendships with others in the body.

    a. Gal. 6.2

    b. Gal. 5.13-14

C. New converts need parental care: ongoing instruction, nurture, and feeding, 1 Thess. 2.7.

1. New baby Christians need the pure milk of the Word of God.

4

a. 1 Pet. 2.2

b. Ps. 19.7-10

c. 1 Cor. 3.2

2. Basic instruction in the dynamics of the Christian life, Eph. 4.20-24

3. Tender, loving care from mature, committed believers, 2 Cor. 12.14

4. Godly authority serves to provide ongoing oversight and care to young and developing converts, Heb. 13.17.

III. Biblical Methods of Follow-Up: the Experience of the Apostles

A. Method one: prevailing prayer on behalf of the new converts, Rom. 1.9-12

1. Variety of intercessions reveal a deep knowledge of the converts

2. Prayers for spiritual insight and illumination, Eph. 1.15ff.

3. Prayer for maturity (edification) and impact (fruitfulness) Col. 1.9-10

B. Method two: immediate, direct personal contact in instruction and care, Acts 20.18-21, 31

1. Adopted the persona of a spiritual parent over their children, 1 Cor. 4.15-16

2. Assumed pastoral responsibility for the ongoing health of the converts

   a. 2 Cor. 11.28

   b. 3 John 1.3-4

3. Cultivated spiritual friendships, Philem. 1.7

C. Method three: sending representatives for encouragement and challenge, 2 Cor. 8.16-23

   1. To provide instruction and guidance, 1 Thess. 3.1-3

   2. To deliver messages of support or exhortation, 1 Cor. 16.10-11

   3. To learn of their mutual estate and condition

      a. Eph. 6.21

      b. Phil. 2.19-24

4

D. Method four: personal correspondence to them, 1 John 5.11-13

   1. Our epistles as follow-up material

   2. Express goal to establish the believers in their particular context

      a. 1 Pet. 5.12

      b. 1 John 2.1

   3. Our epistles themselves provide an argument for diverse kinds of follow-up approaches and materials.

E. Method five: appointing leaders over them, Titus 1.4-5

   1. Connecting believers to churches with godly shepherds is the best follow-up method available.

      a. Acts 14.23

      b. 2 Tim. 2.2

   2. Whatever the method, chances are slim that they will succeed if they are not connected to grounding the new Christians in a healthy body of believers.

a. 1 Cor. 12.21-27

    b. Eph. 4.11-16

Conclusion

» The key to successful urban evangelism is following up new Christians by incorporating them into a local assembly of believers as quickly as possible.

» To follow up new believers in Christ consists of "incorporating new converts into the family of God so they can be equipped to grow in Christ and use their gifts for ministry." This is for the purpose of *maturity* (growing up in Christ) and *fruitfulness* (reproduction in Christ by multiplying disciples).

» Following up new converts is essential because new Christians are vulnerable to attack from the enemy, they need to be reoriented to their new faith in Christ, and they need immediate parental care as little newborns in Christ.

» The New Testament provides five ways that the apostles followed up new converts in Christ, all of which we can still do today. We can prevail for them in intercessory prayer, provide immediate personal contact with them, send personal representatives for encouragement and challenge, maintain regular personal correspondence with them, and ensure that they have solid spiritual leaders over them.

4

Segue 1

Student Questions and Response

Please take as much time as you have available to answer these and other questions on the subject of follow-up and incorporating new believers into the Church. Nothing is as critical for effective evangelism as making provision for the ongoing well being and nurture of those who respond in faith to the Gospel, whether publicly or privately. Remember, be clear and concise in your answers, and where possible, support with Scripture!

1. What is the meaning of follow-up? How is follow-up related to the idea of incorporating new converts into a church as soon as possible?

2. How does the Great Commission (i.e., Matthew 28.18-20) assume some kind of follow-up in the sharing of the Good News with the lost? Why is evangelism that makes no provision for follow-up unacceptable in light of the Great Commission?

3. What is the meaning of the term *edification*, and how does this concept relate to the idea of following up the decisions of new converts as quickly as possible?

4. How does the notion that all believers have been given gifts for the well being of the Church figure into the need for new converts to be incorporated into a local church as soon as possible?

5. What are at least three reasons why new converts must be followed up immediately after their decision to repent and believe in Jesus Christ as risen Lord?

6. Why is spiritual parental and pastoral care so critical for the new believer? Will unpastored Christians thrive in the Lord? Why or why not?

7. What role did prayer and immediate contact play in the apostles' follow-up of new converts?

8. Why did the apostles send personal representatives and write letters to correspond with their new converts? What were their fears for the new believers that motivated these actions?

9. How was the appointment of leaders for the disciples in every city a safeguard for the well being of the new converts in the Lord?

10. What concrete lessons can we learn as we observe the way in which the apostles conducted their evangelism in Christ?

4

Follow-Up and Incorporation

Segment 2: Prompt Incorporation into the Assembly of Believers

Rev. Dr. Don L. Davis

Summary of Segment 2

New believers must be baptized and oriented as new members of the local body of believers as soon as possible. Evangelism makes ample provision to connect every new believer with a healthy, growing body of disciples. In this way, the new converts will be instructed in the Christian basics, taught the importance of pastoral care, and equipped to function as members of the body of Christ.

Our objective for this segment, *Prompt Incorporation into the Assembly of Believers*, is to enable you to see that:

- Baptism is an initial and important sign of faith in Jesus Christ which should take place immediately after one's profession of faith in Jesus.

- Membership is a formal and effective means of affirming one's allegiance to a particular body of Christians (and so demonstrate one's allegiance to Christ).

- New believers must be instructed in the basics of the faith, assurance of salvation, a spiritual walk with God, and living in Christian community.

- Follow-up teaches new converts the importance of pastoral care and oversight , as well as how to function as a full member of the body of Christ.

Video Segment 2 Outline

I. Help Them to Publicly Affirm Their Faith: Baptism and Membership

A. Baptism is a primary and persuasive sign of incorporation into Christ and the Church.

1. Obedience to the command of Christ (baptism is sign of your union and allegiance to Christ)

a. Rom. 6.3-4

b. Matt. 28.19

c. 1 Pet. 3.21

2. Witness and testimony before other believers of your identification with him (baptism as a sign of your new connection with the body of Christ in purpose and mission)

a. 1 Cor. 12.13

b. Gal. 3.27

3. Mark of your connection to a local assembly (baptism as a link to your affiliation with a particular local community of believers)

B. Membership is a formal means of affirming your allegiance to a particular body of Christians, 1 John 2.19-21

1. Why is it important?

a. Public connection to a gathered assembly

b. Recognition by leaders and members of your place in the family

c. A sign of formal adoption: membership as spiritual identity, not merely formal association

2. Membership beats merely visiting in every case!

a. Allows your open and unhindered participation in all forms of body life

b. Draws you into the inner circle of the church's life and decision-making

c. Enables you to take wise advantage of the church's limited store of resources

d. Protects the church at large against the intrusion of "wolves in sheep's clothing"

II. Instruct the New Christian in the Basics of the Christian Life (After-Birth Care).

A. Ground them in the Bible's teaching regarding assurance of salvation, 1 John 5.11-13.

1. The assurance of salvation in Jesus Christ, John 5.24

2. The assurance of forgiveness and cleansing through confession

a. Col. 1.13

b. 1 John 1.5-2.2

3. The assurance of guidance and victory through the Holy Spirit

a. Gal. 5.16

b. Eph. 5.18

c. Rom. 8.1-18

B. Ground them in the Bible's teaching on walking with God (the disciplines of the Christian life), Eph. 4.20-24.

1. Feeding upon the Word of God, 2 Tim. 3.16-17

a. Hearing the Word of God preached, taught, and read

b. Reading through the Bible, Rev. 1.3

c. Memorization of Scripture, Ps. 119.9-11

d. Bible study, 2 Tim. 2.15

e. Meditation upon Scripture, Ps. 1.1-3

2. Prayer and fasting

    a. Luke 18.1

    b. Luke 21.36

    c. Rom. 12.12

    d. Eph. 6.18

    e. Col. 4.2

    f. 1 Pet. 4.7

3. Public and private worship

    a. Ps. 34.1-3

    b. Heb. 13.15

C. Living in Christian community, John 13.34-35; Rom. 12.3-8

1. Becoming a member of the Church, Gal. 3.28

2. Public worship: preaching, praise, and the Lord's Supper, Heb. 10.23-25

3. Living a lifestyle of love, holiness, and generosity

    a. 1 John 4.7-8

    b. Heb. 12.14

    c. 1 Pet. 1.14-16

4. Maintaining good works

    a. Eph. 2.8-10

    b. Titus 2.11-15

5. Sharing faith with others

    a. 1 Pet. 3.15

    b. Rom. 1.16-17

III. Teach New Converts the Importance of Pastoral Care and Oversight.

A. All believers are to be under the authority of undershepherds, Heb. 13.17.

1. They are given to guard believers from harm, Acts 20.28.

2. They are given as models for the faith, Heb. 13.7.

3. They are under God's charge in their duties, 1 Pet. 5.2-3.

B. Obedience and honor to undershepherds as command of the Lord

1. They are co-workers with the Lord, 1 Cor. 3.9.

2. Be in submission to sound leaders, 1 Cor. 16.16.

3. Grant them honor in all things, 1 Tim. 5.17-18.

4. 1 Thess. 5.12-13

C. Benefits from pastoral care and oversight

1. Protection

2. Feeding and nurture

3. Tender, loving care

4. Helping you find your place in ministry

4

IV. Equip Them to Function as a Contributing Member of the Body of Christ.

A. Becoming a member of the body, 1 Cor. 12.13

   1. The importance of baptism, Matt. 28.19

      a. Confession of faith in Christ

      b. Confession of allegiance to the Church's teaching

      c. Confession of connection with the body

   2. The importance of membership

B. Doing one's chores as a family member, 1 Pet. 4.8-11

   1. Bearing one another's burdens, Gal. 6.2

   2. Following the tradition of the apostles, 2 Thess. 3.6

   3. Maintaining a good reputation among the believers

      a. In my home, Eph. 5.22-6.5

b. Among the saints, Gal. 6.10

c. On my job, Eph. 6.5-9

d. In my neighborhood, 1 Pet. 3.15; 1 Cor. 7.17

e. In my community, Matt. 5.14-16

4. Identifying and associating with the believers in my congregation

a. Christ is among us when we gather, Matt. 18.20.

b. Gathering together is a sign of the Spirit's presence, Acts 2.42.

C. Core responsibilities in the body

1. Assembling with the believers: presence, Heb. 10.23-25

2. Giving generously for the well-being of the leaders and teachers, 2 Cor. 8.9

a. Providing for the needs of the saints, 2 Cor. 9.6-8

b. Providing for those who labor among us in the Gospel, Gal. 6.6

c. Contributing to the outreach of the Gospel, Phil. 4.15-17

3. Serving practically in the body together

    a. In service, 1 Thess. 4.9-10

    b. In hospitality, Heb. 13.1-3

D. Using one's gifts as a body member

1. Discovering the gifts of the Spirit, Rom. 12.3-8

    a. Gifts are given by the Holy Spirit for the benefit of the body, 1 Cor. 12.7-10.

    b. Gifts are given to be employed; no saints are to sit on the sidelines, Eph. 4.15-16.

    c. Gifts operate for the upbuilding of the body in love, 1 Pet. 4.10-11.

2. Teaching the new convert to use their gifts and resources for the good of the other members in the body, 1 Cor. 10.23-24

3. Contributing to our witness as a body

    a. Serving our local witness efforts, Phil. 1.27-28

    b. Helping my church reach the world for Christ

        (1) We are called to fight the good fight, 1 Tim. 6.12.

        (2) We must train believers to contend for the faith that has been passed down to us from the apostles, Jude 1.3.

Conclusion

» Baptism is an initial and important sign of faith in Jesus Christ which should take place immediately after one's profession of faith in Jesus.

» Membership is a formal and effective means of affirming one's allegiance to a particular body of Christians (and so demonstrate one's allegiance to Christ).

» New believers must be instructed in the basics of the faith, assurance of salvation, a spiritual walk with God, and living in Christian community.

» Follow-up teaches new converts the importance of pastoral care and oversight , as well as how to function as a full member of the body of Christ.

Segue 2

Student Questions and Response

The following questions were designed to help you review the material in the second video segment. Follow-up is an integral element within all biblical evangelism; when a new Christian accepts Jesus, our responsibility is to ensure that the little newborn believer is fed, cleansed, protected, and cared for with the love of a spiritual parent. This involves primarily our ability to link them to a new body of believers as quickly as possible. Be clear and concise in your answers, and where possible, support with Scripture!

1. In what sense is baptism a primary and persuasive sign of being incorporated (*brought into*) the body of Christ? Can one be saved without baptism? Explain your answer.

2. In what sense does membership in a local assembly protect the newborn Christian from those things and influences which may seek to undermine their new-found faith?

3. Why is the assurance of salvation such an important doctrine for the new believer? What essentially does this doctrine involve?

4

4. Why is it critical to instruct a new believer in the spiritual disciplines, including the corporate disciples of public worship, Bible study, fellowship, and so on? Why isn't merely teaching them the private disciplines enough?

5. What does the Bible teach about believers being under the spiritual oversight of shepherds? What does submission to our leaders mean in a biblical sense?

6. List the obvious spiritual blessings that come to the person who joins themselves to a church *under the leadership of a godly shepherd.*

7. How does one become a member of the body of Christ? How is this similar or unlike "joining a church?"

8. Why are the "one anothers" of the New Testament so important in the ongoing growth and development of the new believer in Christ?

9. What are the core responsibilities we ought to introduce a new convert to immediately after their membership in the body of Christ? What are their "privileges" as a member of the body?

10. Does a new Christian possess any special gift from the Holy Spirit? How are we to equip the new believers to discover and use their gifts in the local church?

Summary of Key Concepts

This lesson focuses upon the importance of incorporating new believers into a local assembly of believers as quickly as possible after their decision to repent and believe in the risen Lord Jesus Christ. God intends for evangelism to result in the multiplying of disciples, and there can be no legitimate discipleship that occurs outside the body of believers. While God has on occasion sustained the believer shackled in the dungeon, the gulag, the prison house, and the pit, his desired way of nurturing Christian discipleship is in the context of believers living in the community of the Spirit under the pastoral oversight of godly shepherds who are feeding and leading God's people.

☞ The key to successful evangelism is following up new Christians by incorporating them into a local assembly of believers as quickly as possible.

☞ To follow up new believers in Christ consists of "incorporating new converts into the family of God so they can be equipped to grow in Christ and use their gifts for ministry." This is for the purpose of *maturity* (growing up in Christ) and *fruitfulness* (reproduction in Christ by multiplying disciples).

↳ New believers must be followed up quickly because they are vulnerable to attack from the enemy, they need to be reoriented to their new faith in Christ, and they need immediate parental care as little newborns in Christ.

↳ The New Testament provides five ways that the apostles followed up new converts in Christ, all of which we can still do today. We can prevail for them in intercessory prayer, provide immediate personal contact with them, send personal representatives for encouragement and challenge, maintain regular personal correspondence with them, and ensure that they have solid spiritual leaders over them.

↳ Baptism is an initial and important sign of faith in Jesus Christ which should take place immediately after one's profession of faith in Jesus.

↳ Membership is a formal and effective means of affirming one's allegiance to a particular body of Christians (and so demonstrate one's allegiance to Christ).

↳ New believers must be instructed in the basics of the faith, assurance of salvation, a spiritual walk with God, and living in Christian community.

↳ Follow-up teaches new converts the importance of pastoral care and oversight, as well as how to function as a full member of the body of Christ.

4

Student Application and Implications

Now is the time for you to discuss with your fellow students your questions about the role of follow-up and incorporation as a necessary element in evangelism and spiritual warfare. If evangelism is the proclamation of deliverance from the kingdom of darkness into the Kingdom of God's beloved Son (cf. Col. 1.13), then evangelism is not merely seeking a decision or asking people to raise their hand, or give some visible sign that they have made a decision in their heart. Rather, it is the outward expression of allegiance to Christ in baptism and membership in a local assembly of believers where Christ is worshiped as Lord of all. In light of these key truths, what particular questions have come to mind as you have discussed these ideas? Maybe some of the questions below might help you form your own, more specific and critical questions.

* Can a person actually claim to be saved if they are unwilling to confess Christ's name before others in the Church? Explain your answer.

* Is it necessary to actually be incorporated into a *local assembly* of believers, or can just a generic commitment to Christianity be sufficient as a sign of authentic repentance and faith in Christ?

* What should we think of evangelistic efforts where no provision is made to incorporate new Christians into the Church?

* Does credible evangelism mean that we incorporate all the converts into *our church* or into *a healthy Christ-honoring church*? If our church is hosting an evangelistic event, should we count on the those who respond coming into our church?

* If we know that the people whom we are called to target will not feel at home in our church, ought we to plant another church, or seek a church for them to be a part? Isn't this going a little too far, having to ensure that every convert be incorporated into a local church?

* What about spontaneous evangelism–sharing the Lord with a person on a plane or bus, or a stranger at an event? Do we even have to try to provide these converts with an assembly to be a part of?

CASE STUDIES

Are They Really Saved?

A person made a commitment to Christ over the television some three years ago, and has never joined a church, or been baptized in Christ. Reasoning that the decision alone has saved him, he feels no need to go to church, and has determined to experience Christ through the teaching and "fellowship" he receives from the radio and television ministers he listens to faithfully. What would you suggest regarding this person's salvation? Are they really saved at all? Are they saved, but untaught regarding the communal nature of the Christian faith? Does only God know for sure? What is your opinion, and why?

No Time to Lose

After a special meeting to win gang members to the Lord, the leaders of the event decide to baptize the individuals as soon as possible. Understanding the importance of baptism and incorporation, they reason that they do not wish to miss a single night, and determine to go back to the church to fill the tank and to baptize the individuals that very night. (They quote the immediacy of the baptisms in Acts as biblical justification for their act tonight). What do you think of their decision? How soon should we encourage new converts to ally themselves to Christ and his Church after their decision?

You Go with Brother Bill

One urban church is so concerned about conserving the fruit of their evangelism that they *assign* new believers to spiritual mentors whose responsibility it is to challenge, encourage, instruct, protect, counsel, and befriend the new convert. While it seems a little tight at first, most of the relationships work out fine, especially since the mentors are under the pastors authority. What do you think of such systems? Should we allow new converts to choose their own "friends" in the church, or do we stand a better chance of saving some of the little lambs if shepherds are actually *assigned to their care* as a part of their spiritual responsibility?

Restatement of the Lesson's Thesis

The key to successful evangelism is following up new Christians by incorporating them into a local assembly of believers as quickly as possible. To follow up new believers in Christ consists of "incorporating new converts into the family of God so they can be equipped to grow in Christ and use their gifts for ministry." This is for the purpose of *maturity* (growing up in Christ) and *fruitfulness* (reproduction in Christ by multiplying disciples). This occurs when we baptize new believers, incorporate them into the local assembly, and instruct them as members of the community, equipping them to live the Christian life as members of the body of Christ.

Resources and Bibliographies

If you are interested in pursuing some of the ideas of *Follow-up and Incorporation*, you might want to give these books a try:

Cosgrove, Francis M., Jr. *Essentials of Discipleship*. Dallas: Roper Press, 1988.

Eims, Leroy. *The Lost Art of Disciplemaking*. Grand Rapids: Zondervan, 1984.

Ortiz, Juan Carlos. *Disciple*. Carol Stream, Ill: Creation House, 1982.

Phillips, Keith. *The Making of a Disciple*. Old Tappan, NJ: Fleming H. Revell Co., 1981.

Wagner, Peter. *Your Spiritual Gifts Can Help Your Church Grow*. Ventura, CA: Regal Books, 1979.

4

You will be responsible to now apply the insights you have learned in your studies in this module in a practicum that you and your mentor agree to. Your ability to think critically regarding the subject of evangelism and spiritual warfare is significant, and its ramifications for your life and ministry are numerous and rich. Just think of all the ways in which the insights you have learned in this module may influence your devotional life, your prayers, your response to your church, your attitude at work, and on and on and on. What is critical for your own development is that you link the insights you have learned directly to some aspect of your personal life, work, and ministry. The ministry project has been specially designed to help make this connection for you, and in the next days you will have the opportunity to share your insights in a real-life, actual ministry environment(s). Pray that God will give you insight into his ways as you share your insights in your projects.

Ministry Connections

Has the Holy Spirit laid any particular issues, persons, situations, or opportunities on your heart that cry out for prayer as a result of your studies in this lesson? Listen to the Lord, and ask him to make plain to you what specific requests or focused supplications and prayers need to be lifted up as a result of what he has revealed in this lesson. Take the time to ponder this, and receive the necessary support in counsel and prayer for what the Spirit has shown you.

Counseling and Prayer

ASSIGNMENTS

No assignment due.

Scripture Memory

No assignment due.

Reading Assignment

Your ministry project and your exegetical project should now be outlined, determined, and accepted by your instructor. Make sure that you plan ahead, so you will not be late in turning in your assignments.

Other Assignments

The final will be a take home exam, and will include questions taken from the first three quizzes, new questions on material drawn from this lesson, and essay questions which will ask for your short answer responses to key integrating questions. Also, you should plan on reciting or writing out the verses memorized

Final Exam Notice

4

for the course on the exam. When you have completed your exam, please notify your mentor and make certain that they get your copy.

. . . .

The Last Word about this Module

Evangelism is proclaiming and demonstrating God's deliverance in the risen Lord Jesus Christ over the devil and the effects of sin and the Curse in the power of the Holy Spirit.

As disciples of Jesus Christ, we have been given the commission to take the Gospel into the entire world (Mark 16.15-16). As we share and show the good news of Christ, men and women, along with boys and girls, will respond in repentance and faith to the Lord's offer. He will bring deliverance to the captives through the power of the Gospel, and all who confess Jesus as Lord and believe that God raised him from the dead will be saved. In our ministry of evangelism, we do battle with the enemy while the Holy Spirit delivers people through the Word of grace in the Gospel of Christ.

Evangelism assumes that we are determined to bring new converts into the very Church of God. Follow-up is absolutely necessary; every new convert must not only be won to Jesus Christ, but, as our definition suggested, each one must be incorporated into the family of God so they can be equipped to grow in Christ and use their gifts for ministry. As the apostles followed up new converts, so we too must do the same.

God demands that our evangelism include follow-up and incorporation into a local assembly of believers. We follow up new believers by helping them publicly affirm their faith by baptism and membership, instructing them in the basics of the Christian life, teaching them the importance of pastoral care and oversight, and equipping them to function as a contributing member of the body of Christ.

Truly, the Gospel is the power of God to salvation to every one who believes. May God give us boldness and clarity as we share the Good News in our communities, under the Spirit's direction!

4

Appendices

APPENDIX 1

The Nicene Creed

Memory Verses ⇩

Rev. 4.11 (ESV) *Worthy are you, our Lord and God, to receive glory and honor and power, for you created all things, and by your will they existed and were created.*

John 1.1 (ESV) *In the beginning was the Word, and the Word was with God, and the Word was God.*

1 Cor.15.3-5 (ESV) *For what I received I passed on to you as of first importance: that Christ died for our sins according to the Scriptures, that he was buried, that he was raised on the third day according to the Scriptures, and that he appeared to Peter, and then to the Twelve.*

Rom. 8.11 (ESV) *If the Spirit of him who raised Jesus from the dead dwells in you, he who raised Christ Jesus from the dead will also give life to your mortal bodies through his Spirit who dwells in you.*

1 Pet. 2.9 (ESV) *But you are a chosen race, a royal priesthood, a holy nation, a people for his own possession, that you may proclaim the excellencies of him who called you out of darkness into his marvelous light.*

1 Thess. 4.16-17 (ESV) *For the Lord himself will descend from heaven with a cry of command, with the voice of an archangel, and with the sound of the trumpet of God. And the dead in Christ will rise first. Then we who are alive, who are left, will be caught up together with them in the clouds to meet the Lord in the air, and so we will always be with the Lord.*

We believe in one God,   *(Deut. 6.4-5; Mark 12.29; 1 Cor. 8.6)*
 the Father Almighty,   *(Gen. 17.1; Dan. 4.35; Matt. 6.9; Eph. 4.6; Rev. 1.8)*
 Maker of heaven and earth   *(Gen 1.1; Isa. 40.28; Rev. 10.6)*
 and of all things visible and invisible.   *(Ps. 148; Rom. 11.36; Rev. 4.11)*

We believe in one Lord Jesus Christ, the only Begotten Son of God,
 begotten of the Father before all ages,
 God from God, Light from Light, True God from True God,
 begotten not created,
 of the same essence as the Father,   *(John 1.1-2; 3.18; 8.58; 14.9-10; 20.28; Col. 1.15, 17; Heb. 1.3-6)*
 through whom all things were made.   *(John 1.3; Col. 1.16)*

Who for us men and for our salvation came down from heaven
 and was incarnate by the Holy Spirit and the virgin Mary
 and became human.   *(Matt. 1.20-23; John 1.14; 6.38; Luke 19.10)*
 Who for us too, was crucified under Pontius Pilate,
 suffered, and was buried.   *(Matt. 27.1-2; Mark 15.24-39, 43-47; Acts 13.29; Rom. 5.8; Heb. 2.10; 13.12)*
 The third day he rose again
 according to the Scriptures,   *(Mark 16.5-7; Luke 24.6-8; Acts 1.3; Rom. 6.9; 10.9; 2 Tim. 2.8)*
 ascended into heaven,
 and is seated at the right hand of the Father.   *(Mark 16.19; Eph. 1.19-20)*
 He will come again in glory
 to judge the living and the dead,
 and his Kingdom will have no end.
  (Isa. 9.7; Matt. 24.30; John 5.22; Acts 1.11; 17.31; Rom. 14.9; 2 Cor. 5.10; 2 Tim. 4.1)

We believe in the Holy Spirit, the Lord and life-giver,
  (Gen. 1.1-2; Job 33.4; Ps. 104.30; 139.7-8; Luke 4.18-19; John 3.5-6; Acts 1.1-2; 1 Cor. 2.11; Rev. 3.22)
 who proceeds from the Father and the Son,   *(John 14.16-18, 26; 15.26; 20.22)*
 who together with the Father and Son
 is worshiped and glorified,   *(Isa. 6.3; Matt. 28.19; 2 Cor. 13.14; Rev. 4.8)*
 who spoke by the prophets.   *(Num. 11.29; Mic. 3.8; Acts 2.17-18; 2 Pet. 1.21)*

We believe in one holy, catholic, and apostolic Church.
  (Matt. 16.18; Eph. 5.25-28; 1 Cor. 1.2; 10.17; 1 Tim. 3.15; Rev. 7.9)

We acknowledge one baptism for the forgiveness of sin,   *(Acts 22.16; 1 Pet. 3.21; Eph. 4.4-5)*
 And we look for the resurrection of the dead
 And the life of the age to come.   *(Isa. 11.6-10; Mic. 4.1-7; Luke 18.29-30; Rev. 21.1-5; 21.22-22.5)*

Amen.

APPENDIX 2

We Believe: Confession of the Nicene Creed (Common Meter*)

Rev. Dr. Don L. Davis, 2007. All Rights Reserved.

* This song is adapted from the Nicene Creed, and set to Common Meter (8.6.8.6.), meaning it can be sung to tunes of the same meter, such as: *O, for a Thousand Tongues to Sing; Alas, and Did My Savior Bleed?; Amazing Grace; All Hail the Power of Jesus' Name; There Is a Fountain; Joy to the World*

The Father God Almighty rules, Maker of earth and heav'n.
Yes, all things seen and those unseen, by him were made, and given!

We hold to one Lord Jesus Christ, God's one and only Son,
Begotten, not created, too, he and our Lord are one!

Begotten from the Father, same, in essence, God and Light;
Through him all things were made by God, in him were given life.

Who for us all, for salvation, came down from heav'n to earth,
Was incarnate by the Spirit's pow'r, and the Virgin Mary's birth.

Who for us too, was crucified, by Pontius Pilate's hand,
Suffered, was buried in the tomb, on third day rose again.

According to the Sacred text all this was meant to be.
Ascended to heav'n, to God's right hand, now seated high in glory.

He'll come again in glory to judge all those alive and dead.
His Kingdom rule shall never end, for he will reign as Head.

We worship God, the Holy Spirit, our Lord, Life-giver known,
With Fath'r and Son is glorified, Who by the prophets spoke.

And we believe in one true Church, God's people for all time,
Cath'lic in scope, and built upon the apostolic line.

Acknowledging one baptism, for forgiv'ness of our sin,
We look for Resurrection day–the dead shall live again.

We look for those unending days, life of the Age to come,
When Christ's great Reign shall come to earth, and God's will shall be done!

APPENDIX 3

The Story of God: Our Sacred Roots

Rev. Dr. Don L. Davis

The Alpha and the Omega	Christus Victor	Come, Holy Spirit	Your Word Is Truth	The Great Confession	His Life in Us	Living in the Way	Reborn to Serve
The LORD God is the source, sustainer, and end of all things in the heavens and earth. All things were formed and exist by his will and for his eternal glory, the triune God, Father, Son, and Holy Spirit. Rom. 11.36.							
THE TRIUNE GOD'S UNFOLDING DRAMA — God's Self-Revelation in Creation, Israel, and Christ				THE CHURCH'S PARTICIPATION IN GOD'S UNFOLDING DRAMA — Fidelity to the Apostolic Witness to Christ and His Kingdom			
	The Objective Foundation: The Sovereign Love of God — *God's Narration of His Saving Work in Christ*			The Subjective Practice: Salvation by Grace through Faith — *The Redeemed's Joyous Response to God's Saving Work in Christ*			
The Author of the Story	*The Champion of the Story*	*The Interpreter of the Story*	*The Testimony of the Story*	*The People of the Story*	*Re-enactment of the Story*	*Embodiment of the Story*	*Continuation of the Story*
The Father as Director	Jesus as Lead Actor	The Spirit as Narrator	Scripture as Script	As Saints, Confessors	As Worshipers, Ministers	As Followers, Sojourners	As Servants, Ambassadors
Christian Worldview	Communal Identity	Spiritual Experience	Biblical Authority	Orthodox Theology	Priestly Worship	Congregational Discipleship	Kingdom Witness
Theistic and Trinitarian Vision	Christ-centered Foundation	Spirit-Indwelt and -Filled Community	Canonical and Apostolic Witness	Ancient Creedal Affirmation of Faith	Weekly Gathering in Christian Assembly	Corporate, Ongoing Spiritual Formation	Active Agents of the Reign of God
Sovereign Willing	Messianic Representing	Divine Comforting	Inspired Testifying	Truthful Retelling	Joyful Excelling	Faithful Indwelling	Hopeful Compelling
Creator — True Maker of the Cosmos	Recapitulation — Typos and Fulfillment of the Covenant	Life-Giver — Regeneration and Adoption	Divine Inspiration — God-breathed Word	The Confession of Faith — Union with Christ	Song and Celebration — Historical Recitation	Pastoral Oversight — Shepherding the Flock	Explicit Unity — Love for the Saints
Owner — Sovereign Disposer of Creation	Revealer — Incarnation of the Word	Teacher — Illuminator of the Truth	Sacred History — Historical Record	Baptism into Christ — Communion of Saints	Homilies and Teachings — Prophetic Proclamation	Shared Spirituality — Common Journey through the Spiritual Disciplines	Radical Hospitality — Evidence of God's Kingdom Reign
Ruler — Blessed Controller of All Things	Redeemer — Reconciler of All Things	Helper — Endowment and the Power	Biblical Theology — Divine Commentary	The Rule of Faith — Apostles' Creed and Nicene Creed	The Lord's Supper — Dramatic Re-enactment	Embodiment — Anamnesis and Prolepsis through the Church Year	Extravagant Generosity — Good Works
Covenant Keeper — Faithful Promisor	Restorer — Christ, the Victor over the powers of evil	Guide — Divine Presence and Shekinah	Spiritual Food — Sustenance for the Journey	The Vincentian Canon — Ubiquity, antiquity, universality	Eschatological Foreshadowing — The Already/Not Yet	Effective Discipling — Spiritual Formation in the Believing Assembly	Evangelical Witness — Making Disciples of All People Groups

APPENDIX 4

The Theology of Christus Victor

A Christ-Centered Biblical Motif for Integrating and Renewing the Urban Church

Rev. Dr. Don L. Davis

	The Promised Messiah	The Word Made Flesh	The Son of Man	The Suffering Servant	The Lamb of God	The Victorious Conqueror	The Reigning Lord in Heaven	The Bridegroom and Coming King
Biblical Framework	Israel's hope of Yahweh's anointed who would redeem his people	In the person of Jesus of Nazareth, the Lord has come to the world	As the promised king and divine Son of Man, Jesus reveals the Father's glory and salvation to the world	As Inaugurator of the Kingdom of God, Jesus demonstrates God's reign present through his words, wonders, and works	As both High Priest and Paschal Lamb, Jesus offers himself to God as a sacrifice for sin	In his resurrection from the dead and ascension to God's right hand, Jesus is proclaimed as Victor over the power of sin and death	Now reigning at God's right hand till his enemies are made his footstool, Jesus pours out his benefits on his body	Soon the risen and ascended Lord will return to gather his Bride, the Church, and consummate his work
Scripture References	Isa. 9.6-7 Jer. 23.5-6 Isa. 11.1-10	John 1.14-18 Matt. 1.20-23 Phil. 2.6-8	Matt. 2.1-11 Num. 24.17 Luke 1.78-79	Mark 1.14-15 Matt. 12.25-30 Luke 17.20-21	2 Cor. 5.18-21 Isa. 52-53 John 1.29	Eph. 1.16-23 Phil. 2.5-11 Col. 1.15-20	1 Cor. 15.25 Eph. 4.15-16 Acts. 2.32-36	Rom. 14.7-9 Rev. 5.9-13 1 Thess. 4.13-18
Jesus' History	The pre-incarnate, only begotten Son of God in glory	His conception by the Spirit, and birth to Mary	His manifestation to the Magi and to the world	His teaching, exorcisms, miracles, and mighty works among the people	His suffering, crucifixion, death, and burial	His resurrection, with appearances to his witnesses, and his ascension to the Father	The sending of the Holy Spirit and his gifts, and Christ's session in heaven at the Father's right hand	His soon return from heaven to earth as Lord and Christ: the Second Coming
Description	The biblical promise for the seed of Abraham, the prophet like Moses, the son of David	In the Incarnation, God has come to us; Jesus reveals to humankind the Father's glory in fullness	In Jesus, God has shown his salvation to the entire world, including the Gentiles	In Jesus, the promised Kingdom of God has come visibly to earth, demonstrating his binding of Satan and rescinding the Curse	As God's perfect Lamb, Jesus offers himself up to God as a sin offering on behalf of the entire world	In his resurrection and ascension, Jesus destroyed death, disarmed Satan, and rescinded the Curse	Jesus is installed at the Father's right hand as Head of the Church, Firstborn from the dead, and supreme Lord in heaven	As we labor in his harvest field in the world, so we await Christ's return, the fulfillment of his promise
Church Year	Advent	Christmas	Season after Epiphany Baptism and Transfiguration	Lent	Holy Week Passion	Eastertide Easter, Ascension Day, Pentecost	Season after Pentecost Trinity Sunday	Season after Pentecost All Saints Day, Reign of Christ the King
Spiritual Formation	*The Coming of Christ* As we await his Coming, let us proclaim and affirm the hope of Christ	*The Birth of Christ* O Word made flesh, let us every heart prepare him room to dwell	*The Manifestation of Christ* Divine Son of Man, show the nations your salvation and glory	*The Ministry of Christ* In the person of Christ, the power of the reign of God has come to earth and to the Church	*The Suffering and Death of Christ* May those who share the Lord's death be resurrected with him	*The Resurrection and Ascension of Christ* Let us participate by faith in the victory of Christ over the power of sin, Satan, and death	*The Heavenly Session of Christ* Come, indwell us, Holy Spirit, and empower us to advance Christ's Kingdom in the world	*The Reign of Christ* We live and work in expectation of his soon return, seeking to please him in all things

APPENDIX 5

Christus Victor
An Integrated Vision for the Christian Life
Rev. Dr. Don L. Davis

For the Church

- The Church is the primary extension of Jesus in the world
- Ransomed treasure of the victorious, risen Christ
- *Laos:* The people of God
- God's new creation: presence of the future
- Locus and agent of the Already/Not Yet Kingdom

For Theology and Doctrine

- The authoritative Word of Christ's victory: the Apostolic Tradition: the Holy Scriptures
- Theology as commentary on the grand narrative of God
- *Christus Victor* as core theological framework for meaning in the world
- The Nicene Creed: the Story of God's triumphant grace

For Spirituality

- The Holy Spirit's presence and power in the midst of God's people
- Sharing in the disciplines of the Spirit
- Gatherings, lectionary, liturgy, and our observances in the Church Year
- Living the life of the risen Christ in the rhythm of our ordinary lives

For Gifts

- God's gracious endowments and benefits from *Christus Victor*
- Pastoral offices to the Church
- The Holy Spirit's sovereign dispensing of the gifts
- Stewardship: divine, diverse gifts for the common good

Christus Victor

Destroyer of Evil and Death Restorer of Creation Victor o'er Hades and Sin Crusher of Satan

For Worship

- People of the Resurrection: unending celebration of the people of God
- Remembering, participating in the Christ event in our worship
- Listen and respond to the Word
- Transformed at the Table, the Lord's Supper
- The presence of the Father through the Son in the Spirit

For Evangelism and Mission

- Evangelism as unashamed declaration and demonstration of *Christus Victor* to the world
- The Gospel as Good News of kingdom pledge
- We proclaim God's Kingdom come in the person of Jesus of Nazareth
- The Great Commission: go to all people groups making disciples of Christ and his Kingdom
- Proclaiming Christ as Lord and Messiah

For Justice and Compassion

- The gracious and generous expressions of Jesus through the Church
- The Church displays the very life of the Kingdom
- The Church demonstrates the very life of the Kingdom of heaven right here and now
- Having freely received, we freely give (no sense of merit or pride)
- Justice as tangible evidence of the Kingdom come

APPENDIX 6

Old Testament Witness to Christ and His Kingdom

Rev. Dr. Don L. Davis

Christ Is Seen in the OT's:	Covenant Promise and Fulfillment	Moral Law	Christophanies	Typology	Tabernacle, Festival, and Levitical Priesthood	Messianic Prophecy	Salvation Promises
Passage	Gen. 12.1-3	Matt. 5.17-18	John 1.18	1 Cor. 15.45	Heb. 8.1-6	Mic. 5.2	Isa. 9.6-7
Example	The Promised Seed of the Abrahamic covenant	The Law given on Mount Sinai	Commander of the Lord's army	Jonah and the great fish	Melchizedek, as both High Priest and King	The Lord's Suffering Servant	Righteous Branch of David
Christ As	Seed of the woman	The Prophet of God	God's present Revelation	Antitype of God's drama	Our eternal High Priest	The coming Son of Man	Israel's Redeemer and King
Where Illustrated	Galatians	Matthew	John	Matthew	Hebrews	Luke and Acts	John and Revelation
Exegetical Goal	To see Christ as heart of God's sacred drama	To see Christ as fulfillment of the Law	To see Christ as God's revealer	To see Christ as antitype of divine typos	To see Christ in the Temple cultus	To see Christ as true Messiah	To see Christ as coming King
How Seen in the NT	As fulfillment of God's sacred oath	As telos of the Law	As full, final, and superior revelation	As substance behind the historical shadows	As reality behind the rules and roles	As the Kingdom made present	As the One who will rule on David's throne
Our Response in Worship	God's veracity and faithfulness	God's perfect righteousness	God's presence among us	God's inspired Scripture	God's ontology: his realm as primary and determinative	God's anointed servant and mediator	God's resolve to restore his kingdom authority
How God Is Vindicated	God does not lie; he's true to his word	Jesus fulfills all righteousness	God's fulness is revealed to us in Jesus of Nazareth	The Spirit spoke by the prophets	The Lord has provided a mediator for humankind	Every jot and tittle written of him will occur	Evil will be put down, creation restored, under his reign

APPENDIX 7

Summary Outline of the Scriptures

Rev. Dr. Don L. Davis

1. GENESIS - Beginnings
   a. Adam
   b. Noah
   c. Abraham
   d. Isaac
   e. Jacob
   f. Joseph

2. EXODUS - Redemption, (out of)
   a. Slavery
   b. Deliverance
   c. Law
   d. Tabernacle

3. LEVITICUS - Worship and Fellowship
   a. Offerings, sacrifices
   b. Priests
   c. Feasts, festivals

4. NUMBERS - Service and Walk
   a. Organized
   b. Wanderings

5. DEUTERONOMY - Obedience
   a. Moses reviews history and law
   b. Civil and social laws
   c. Palestinian Covenant
   d. Moses' blessing and death

6. JOSHUA - Redemption (into)
   a. Conquer the land
   b. Divide up the land
   c. Joshua's farewell

7. JUDGES - God's Deliverance
   a. Disobedience and judgment
   b. Israel's twelve judges
   c. Lawless conditions

8. RUTH - Love
   a. Ruth chooses
   b. Ruth works
   c. Ruth waits
   d. Ruth rewarded

9. 1 SAMUEL - Kings, Priestly Perspective
   a. Eli
   b. Samuel
   c. Saul
   d. David

10. 2 SAMUEL - David
    a. King of Judah
       (9 years - Hebron)
    b. King of all Israel
       (33 years - Jerusalem)

11. 1 KINGS - Solomon's Glory, Kingdom's Decline
    a. Solomon's glory
    b. Kingdom's decline
    c. Elijah the prophet

12. 2 KINGS- Divided Kingdom
    a. Elisha
    b. Israel (N. Kingdom falls)
    c. Judah (S. Kingdom falls)

13. 1 CHRONICLES - David's Temple Arrangements
    a. Genealogies
    b. End of Saul's reign
    c. Reign of David
    d. Temple preparations

14. 2 CHRONICLES - Temple and Worship Abandoned
    a. Solomon
    b. Kings of Judah

15. EZRA - The Minority (Remnant)
    a. First return from exile - Zerubbabel
    b. Second return from exile - Ezra (priest)

16. NEHEMIAH - Rebuilding by Faith
    a. Rebuild walls
    b. Revival
    c. Religious reform

17. ESTHER - Female Savior
    a. Esther
    b. Haman
    c. Mordecai
    d. Deliverance: Feast of Purim

18. JOB - Why the Righteous Suffer
    a. Godly Job
    b. Satan's attack
    c. Four philosophical friends
    d. God lives

19. PSALMS - Prayer and Praise
    a. Prayers of David
    b. Godly suffer; deliverance
    c. God deals with Israel
    d. Suffering of God's people - end with the Lord's reign
    e. The Word of God (Messiah's suffering and glorious return)

20. PROVERBS - Wisdom
    a. Wisdom versus folly
    b. Solomon
    c. Solomon - Hezekiah
    d. Agur
    e. Lemuel

21. ECCLESIASTES - Vanity
    a. Experimentation
    b. Observation
    c. Consideration

22. SONG OF SOLOMON - Love Story

23. ISAIAH - The Justice (Judgment) and Grace (Comfort) of God
    a. Prophecies of punishment
    b. History
    c. Prophecies of blessing

24. JEREMIAH - Judah's Sin Leads to Babylonian Captivity
    a. Jeremiah's call; empowered
    b. Judah condemned; predicted Babylonian captivity
    c. Restoration promised
    d. Prophesied judgment inflicted
    e. Prophesies against Gentiles
    f. Summary of Judah's captivity

25. LAMENTATIONS - Lament over Jerusalem
    a. Affliction of Jerusalem
    b. Destroyed because of sin
    c. The prophet's suffering
    d. Present desolation versus past splendor
    e. Appeal to God for mercy

26. EZEKIEL - Israel's Captivity and Restoration
    a. Judgment on Judah and Jerusalem
    b. Judgment on Gentile nations
    c. Israel restored; Jerusalem's future glory

27. DANIEL - The Time of the Gentiles
    a. History; Nebuchadnezzar, Belshazzar, Daniel
    b. Prophecy

28. HOSEA - Unfaithfulness
    a. Unfaithfulness
    b. Punishment
    c. Restoration

29. JOEL - The Day of the Lord
    a. Locust plague
    b. Events of the future day of the Lord
    c. Order of the future day of the Lord

30. AMOS - God Judges Sin
    a. Neighbors judged
    b. Israel judged
    c. Visions of future judgment
    d. Israel's past judgment blessings

31. OBADIAH - Edom's Destruction
    a. Destruction prophesied
    b. Reasons for destruction
    c. Israel's future blessing

32. JONAH - Gentile Salvation
    a. Jonah disobeys
    b. Other suffer
    c. Jonah punished
    d. Jonah obeys; thousands saved
    e. Jonah displeased, no love for souls

33. MICAH - Israel's Sins, Judgment, and Restoration
    a. Sin and judgment
    b. Grace and future restoration
    c. Appeal and petition

34. NAHUM - Nineveh Condemned
    a. God hates sin
    b. Nineveh's doom prophesied
    c. Reasons for doom

35. HABAKKUK - The Just Shall Live by Faith
    a. Complaint of Judah's unjudged sin
    b. Chaldeans will punish
    c. Complaint of Chaldeans' wickedness
    d. Punishment promised
    e. Prayer for revival; faith in God

36. ZEPHANIAH - Babylonian Invasion Prefigures the Day of the Lord
    a. Judgment on Judah foreshadows the Great Day of the Lord
    b. Judgment on Jerusalem and neighbors foreshadows final judgment of all nations
    c. Israel restored after judgments

37. HAGGAI - Rebuild the Temple
    a. Negligence
    b. Courage
    c. Separation
    d. Judgment

38. ZECHARIAH - Two Comings of Christ
    a. Zechariah's vision
    b. Bethel's question; Jehovah's answer
    c. Nation's downfall and salvation

39. MALACHI - Neglect
    a. The priest's sins
    b. The people's sins
    c. The faithful few

Summary Outline of the Scriptures (continued)

1. MATTHEW - Jesus the King a. The Person of the King b. The Preparation of the King c. The Propaganda of the King d. The Program of the King e. The Passion of the King f. The Power of the King	**7. 1 CORINTHIANS - The Lordship of Christ** a. Salutation and thanksgiving b. Conditions in the Corinthian body c. Concerning the Gospel d. Concerning collections	**14. 2 THESSALONIANS - The Second Coming of Christ** a. Persecution of believers now; judgment of unbelievers hereafter (at coming of Christ) b. Program of the world in connection with the coming of Christ c. Practical issues associated with the coming of Christ	**21. 1 PETER - Christian Hope in the Time of Persecution and Trial** a. Suffering and security of believers b. Suffering and the Scriptures c. Suffering and the sufferings of Christ d. Suffering and the Second Coming of Christ
2. MARK - Jesus the Servant a. John introduces the Servant b. God the Father identifies the Servant c. The temptation initiates the Servant d. Work and word of the Servant e. Death, burial, resurrection	**8. 2 CORINTHIANS - The Ministry in the Church** a. The comfort of God b. Collection for the poor c. Calling of the Apostle Paul	**15. 1 TIMOTHY - Government and Order in the Local Church** a. The faith of the Church b. Public prayer and women's place in the Church c. Officers in the Church d. Apostasy in the Church e. Duties of the officer of the Church	**22. 2 PETER - Warning Against False Teachers** a. Addition of Christian graces gives assurance b. Authority of the Scriptures c. Apostasy brought in by false testimony d. Attitude toward Return of Christ: test for apostasy e. Agenda of God in the world f. Admonition to believers
3. LUKE - Jesus Christ the Perfect Man a. Birth and family of the Perfect Man b. Testing of the Perfect Man; hometown c. Ministry of the Perfect Man d. Betrayal, trial, and death of the Perfect Man e. Resurrection of the Perfect Man	**9. GALATIANS - Justification by Faith** a. Introduction b. Personal - Authority of the Apostle and glory of the Gospel c. Doctrinal - Justification by faith d. Practical - Sanctification by the Holy Spirit e. Autographed conclusion and exhortation	**16. 2 TIMOTHY - Loyalty in the Days of Apostasy** a. Afflictions of the Gospel b. Active in service c. Apostasy coming; authority of the Scriptures d. Allegiance to the Lord	**23. 1 JOHN - The Family of God** a. God is Light b. God is Love c. God is Life

4. JOHN - Jesus Christ is God
a. Prologue - the Incarnation
b. Introduction
c. Witness of Jesus to his Apostles
d. Passion - witness to the world
e. Epilogue
	10. EPHESIANS - The Church of Jesus Christ
	a. Doctrinal - the heavenly calling of the Church
	  A Body
	  A Temple
	  A Mystery
	b. Practical - The earthly conduct of the Church
	  A New Man
	  A Bride
	  An Army
		17. TITUS - The Ideal New Testament Church
		a. The Church is an organization
		b. The Church is to teach and preach the Word of God
		c. The Church is to perform good works
			24. 2 JOHN - Warning against Receiving Deceivers
			a. Walk in truth
			b. Love one another
			c. Receive not deceivers
			d. Find joy in fellowship

5. ACTS - The Holy Spirit Working in the Church a. The Lord Jesus at work by the Holy Spirit through the Apostles at Jerusalem b. In Judea and Samaria c. To the uttermost parts of the Earth	**11. PHILIPPIANS - Joy in the Christian Life** a. Philosophy for Christian living b. Pattern for Christian living c. Prize for Christian living d. Power for Christian living	**18. PHILEMON - Reveal Christ's Love and Teach Brotherly Love** a. Genial greeting to Philemon and family b. Good reputation of Philemon c. Gracious plea for Onesimus d. Guiltless illustration of Imputation e. General and personal requests	**25. 3 JOHN - Admonition to Receive True Believers** a. Gaius, brother in the Church b. Diotrephes c. Demetrius
6. ROMANS - The Righteousness of God a. Salutation b. Sin and salvation c. Sanctification d. Struggle e. Spirit-filled living f. Security of salvation g. Segregation h. Sacrifice and service i. Separation and salutation	**12. COLOSSIANS - Christ the Fullness of God** a. Doctrinal - In Christ believers are made full b. Practical - Christ's life poured out in believers, and through them	**19. HEBREWS - The Superiority of Christ** a. Doctrinal - Christ is better than the Old Testament economy b. Practical - Christ brings better benefits and duties	**26. JUDE - Contending for the Faith** a. Occasion of the epistle b. Occurrences of apostasy c. Occupation of believers in the days of apostasy
	13. 1 THESSALONIANS - The Second Coming of Christ: a. Is an inspiring hope b. Is a working hope c. Is a purifying hope d. Is a comforting hope e. Is a rousing, stimulating hope	**20. JAMES - Ethics of Christianity** a. Faith tested b. Difficulty of controlling the tongue c. Warning against worldliness d. Admonitions in view of the Lord's coming	**27. REVELATION - The Unveiling of Christ Glorified** a. The person of Christ in glory b. The possession of Jesus Christ - the Church in the World c. The program of Jesus Christ - the scene in Heaven d. The seven seals e. The seven trumpets f. Important persons in the last days g. The seven vials h. The fall of Babylon i. The eternal state

APPENDIX 8

From Before to Beyond Time:

The Plan of God and Human History

Adapted from: Suzanne de Dietrich. **God's Unfolding Purpose.** *Philadelphia: Westminster Press, 1976.*

I. Before Time (Eternity Past) 1 Cor. 2.7
   A. The Eternal Triune God
   B. God's Eternal Purpose
   C. The Mystery of Iniquity
   D. The Principalities and Powers

II. Beginning of Time (Creation and Fall) Gen. 1.1
   A. Creative Word
   B. Humanity
   C. Fall
   D. Reign of Death and First Signs of Grace

III. Unfolding of Time (God's Plan Revealed Through Israel) Gal. 3.8
   A. Promise (Patriarchs)
   B. Exodus and Covenant at Sinai
   C. Promised Land
   D. The City, the Temple, and the Throne (Prophet, Priest, and King)
   E. Exile
   F. Remnant

IV. Fullness of Time (Incarnation of the Messiah) Gal. 4.4-5
   A. The King Comes to His Kingdom
   B. The Present Reality of His Reign
   C. The Secret of the Kingdom: the Already and the Not Yet
   D. The Crucified King
   E. The Risen Lord

V. The Last Times (The Descent of the Holy Spirit) Acts 2.16-18
   A. Between the Times: the Church as Foretaste of the Kingdom
   B. The Church as Agent of the Kingdom
   C. The Conflict Between the Kingdoms of Darkness and Light

VI. The Fulfillment of Time (The Second Coming) Matt. 13.40-43
   A. The Return of Christ
   B. Judgment
   C. The Consummation of His Kingdom

VII. Beyond Time (Eternity Future) 1 Cor. 15.24-28
   A. Kingdom Handed Over to God the Father
   B. God as All in All

From Before to Beyond Time
Scriptures for Major Outline Points

I. Before Time (Eternity Past)

1 Cor. 2.7 (ESV) - But we impart a secret and hidden wisdom of God, *which God decreed before the ages* for our glory (cf. Titus 1.2).

II. Beginning of Time (Creation and Fall)

Gen. 1.1 (ESV) - *In the beginning*, God created the heavens and the earth.

III. Unfolding of Time (God's Plan Revealed Through Israel)

Gal. 3.8 (ESV) - And the Scripture, foreseeing that God would justify the Gentiles by faith, *preached the Gospel beforehand to Abraham*, saying, "In you shall all the nations be blessed" (cf. Rom. 9.4-5).

IV. Fullness of Time (The Incarnation of the Messiah)

Gal. 4.4-5 (ESV) - *But when the fullness of time had come*, God sent forth his Son, born of woman, born under the law, to redeem those who were under the law, so that we might receive adoption as sons.

V. The Last Times (The Descent of the Holy Spirit)

Acts 2.16-18 (ESV) - But this is what was uttered through the prophet Joel: "'*And in the last days it shall be*,' God declares, 'that I will pour out my Spirit on all flesh, and your sons and your daughters shall prophesy, and your young men shall see visions, and your old men shall dream dreams; even on my male servants and female servants in those days I will pour out my Spirit, and they shall prophesy.'"

VI. The Fulfillment of Time (The Second Coming)

Matt. 13.40-43 (ESV) - Just as the weeds are gathered and burned with fire, *so will it be at the close of the age*. The Son of Man will send his angels, and they will gather out of his kingdom all causes of sin and all lawbreakers, and throw them into the fiery furnace. In that place there will be weeping and gnashing of teeth. Then the righteous will shine like the sun in the Kingdom of their Father. He who has ears, let him hear.

VII. Beyond Time (Eternity Future)

1 Cor. 15.24-28 (ESV) - Then comes the end, when he delivers the Kingdom to God the Father after destroying every rule and every authority and power. For he must reign until he has put all his enemies under his feet. The last enemy to be destroyed is death. For "God has put all things in subjection under his feet." But when it says, "all things are put in subjection," it is plain that he is excepted who put all things in subjection under him. When all things are subjected to him, then the Son himself will also be subjected to him who put all things in subjection under him, that God may be all in all.

APPENDIX 9
"There Is a River"

Identifying the Streams of a Revitalized Authentic Christian Community in the City[1]

Rev. Dr. Don L. Davis • Psalm 46.4 (ESV) - There is a river whose streams make glad the city of God, the holy habitation of the Most High.

Tributaries of Authentic Historic Biblical Faith			
Recognized Biblical Identity	Revived Urban Spirituality	Reaffirmed Historical Connectivity	Refocused Kingdom Authority
The Church Is **One**	The Church Is **Holy**	The Church Is **Catholic**	The Church Is **Apostolic**
A Call to Biblical Fidelity Recognizing the Scriptures as the anchor and foundation of the Christian faith and practice	A Call to the Freedom, Power, and Fullness of the Holy Spirit Walking in the holiness, power, gifting, and liberty of the Holy Spirit in the body of Christ	A Call to Historic Roots and Continuity Confessing the common historical identity and continuity of authentic Christian faith	A Call to the Apostolic Faith Affirming the apostolic tradition as the authoritative ground of the Christian hope
A Call to Messianic Kingdom Identity Rediscovering the story of the promised Messiah and his Kingdom in Jesus of Nazareth	A Call to Live as Sojourners and Aliens as the People of God Defining authentic Christian discipleship as faithful membership among God's people	A Call to Affirm and Express the Global Communion of Saints Expressing cooperation and collaboration with all other believers, both local and global	A Call to Representative Authority Submitting joyfully to God's gifted servants in the Church as undershepherds of true faith
A Call to Creedal Affinity Embracing the Nicene Creed as the shared rule of faith of historic orthodoxy	A Call to Liturgical, Sacramental, and Catechetical Vitality Experiencing God's presence in the context of the Word, sacrament, and instruction	A Call to Radical Hospitality and Good Works Expressing kingdom love to all, and especially to those of the household of faith	A Call to Prophetic and Holistic Witness Proclaiming Christ and his Kingdom in word and deed to our neighbors and all peoples

[1] This schema is an adaptation and is based on the insights of the **Chicago Call** statement of May 1977, where various leading evangelical scholars and practitioners met to discuss the relationship of modern evangelicalism to the historic Christian faith.

APPENDIX 10

A Schematic for a Theology of the Kingdom and the Church

The Urban Ministry Institute

The Reign of the One, True, Sovereign, and Triune God, the LORD God, Yahweh, God the Father, Son, and Holy Spirit

The Father	The Son	The Spirit
Love - 1 John 4.8 Maker of heaven and earth and of all things visible and invisible	Faith - Heb. 12.2 Prophet, Priest, and King	Hope - Rom. 15.13 Lord of the Church

Creation	Kingdom	Church
All that exists through the creative action of God.	The Reign of God expressed in the rule of his Son Jesus the Messiah.	The one, holy, apostolic community which functions as a witness to (Acts 28.31) and a foretaste of (Col. 1.12; James 1.18; 1 Pet. 2.9; Rev. 1.6) the Kingdom of God.

	Rom. 8.18-21 →	**Freedom** (Slavery)	*The Church is an Apostolic Community Where the Word is Rightly Preached, Therefore it is a Community of:*

The eternal God, sovereign in power, infinite in wisdom, perfect in holiness, and steadfast in love, is the source and goal of all things.

Jesus answered them, "Truly, truly, I say to you, everyone who commits sin is a slave to sin. The slave does not remain in the house forever; the son remains forever. So if the Son sets you free, you will be free indeed." - John 8.34-36 (ESV)

Calling - For freedom Christ has set us free; stand firm therefore, and do not submit again to a yoke of slavery. - Gal. 5.1 (ESV) (cf. Rom. 8.28-30; 1 Cor. 1.26-31; Eph. 1.18; 2 Thess. 2.13-14; Jude 1.1)

Faith - ". . . for unless you believe that I am he you will die in your sins" . . . . So Jesus said to the Jews who had believed in him, "If you abide in my word, you are truly my disciples, and you will know the truth, and the truth will set you free." - John 8.24b, 31-32 (ESV) (cf. Ps. 119.45; Rom. 1.17; 5.1-2; Eph. 2.8-9; 2 Tim. 1.13-14; Heb. 2.14-15; James 1.25)

Witness - The Spirit of the Lord is upon me, because he has anointed me to proclaim good news to the poor. He has sent me to proclaim liberty to the captives and recovering of sight to the blind, to set at liberty those who are oppressed, to proclaim the year of the Lord's favor. - Luke 4.18-19 (ESV) (cf. Lev. 25.10; Prov. 31.8; Matt. 4.17; 28.18-20; Mark 13.10; Acts 1.8; 8.4, 12; 13.1-3; 25.20; 28.30-31)

O, the depth of the riches and wisdom and knowledge of God! How unsearchable are his judgments, and how inscrutable his ways! For who has known the mind of the Lord, or who has been his counselor? Or who has ever given a gift to him, that he might be repaid?" For from him and through him and to him are all things. To him be glory forever! Amen! - Rom. 11.33-36 (ESV) (cf. 1 Cor. 15.23-28; Rev.)

	Rev. 21.1-5 →	**Wholeness** (Sickness)	*The Church is One Community Where the Sacraments are Rightly Administered, Therefore it is a Community of:*

But he was wounded for our transgressions; he was crushed for our iniquities; upon him was the chastisement that brought us peace, and with his stripes we are healed. - Isa. 53.5 (ESV)

Worship - You shall serve the Lord your God, and he will bless your bread and your water, and I will take sickness away from among you. - Exod. 23.25 (ESV) (cf. Ps. 147.1-3; Heb. 12.28; Col. 3.16; Rev. 15.3-4; 19.5)

Covenant - And the Holy Spirit also bears witness to us; for after the saying, "This is the covenant that I will make with them after those days, declares the Lord: I will put my laws on their hearts, and write them on their minds," then he adds, "I will remember their sins and their lawless deeds no more." - Heb. 10.15-17 (ESV) (cf. Isa. 54.10-17; Ezek. 34.25-31; 37.26-27; Mal. 2.4-5; Luke 22.20; 2 Cor. 3.6; Col. 3.15; Heb. 8.7-13; 12.22-24; 13.20-21)

Presence - In him you also are being built together into a dwelling place for God by his Spirit. - Eph. 2.22 (ESV) (cf. Exod. 40.34-38; Ezek. 48.35; Matt. 18.18-20)

	Isa. 11.6-9 →	**Justice** (Selfishness)	*The Church is a Holy Community Where Discipline is Rightly Ordered, Therefore it is a Community of:*

Behold, my servant whom I have chosen, my beloved with whom my soul is well pleased. I will put my Spirit upon him, and he will proclaim justice to the Gentiles. He will not quarrel or cry aloud, nor will anyone hear his voice in the streets; a bruised reed he will not break, and a smoldering wick he will not quench, until he brings justice to victory. - Matt. 12.18-20 (ESV)

Reconciliation - For he himself is our peace, who has made us both one and has broken down in his flesh the dividing wall of hostility by abolishing the law of commandments and ordinances, that he might create in himself one new man in place of the two, so making peace, and might reconcile us both to God in one body through the cross, thereby killing the hostility. And he came and preached peace to you who were far off and peace to those who were near. For through him we both have access in one Spirit to the Father. - Eph. 2.14-18 (ESV) (cf. Exod. 23.4-9; Lev. 19.34; Deut. 10.18-19; Ezek. 22.29; Mic. 6.8; 2 Cor. 5.16-21)

Suffering - Since therefore Christ suffered in the flesh, arm yourselves with the same way of thinking, for whoever has suffered in the flesh has ceased from sin, so as to live for the rest of the time in the flesh no longer for human passions but for the will of God. - 1 Pet. 4.1-2 (ESV) (cf. Luke 6.22; 10.3; Rom. 8.17; 2 Tim. 2.3; 3.12; 1 Pet. 2.20-24; Heb. 5.8; 13.11-14)

Service - But Jesus called them to him and said, "You know that the rulers of the Gentiles lord it over them, and their great ones exercise authority over them. It shall not be so among you. But whoever would be great among you must be your servant, and whoever would be first among you must be your slave even as the Son of Man came not to be served but to serve, and to give his life as a ransom for many." - Matt. 20.25-28 (ESV) (cf. 1 John 4.16-18; Gal. 2.10)

APPENDIX 11

Living in the Already and the Not Yet Kingdom

Rev. Dr. Don L. Davis

The Spirit: The pledge of the inheritance (**arrabon**)
The Church: The foretaste (**aparche**) of the Kingdom
"In Christ": The rich life (**en Christos**) we share as citizens of the Kingdom

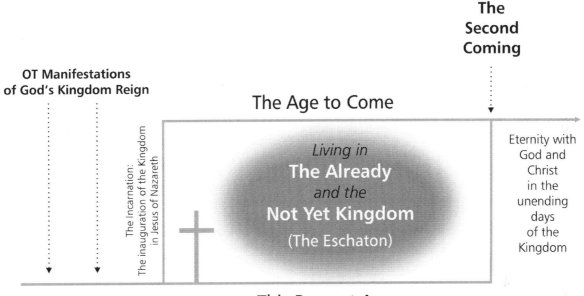

Internal enemy: The flesh (*sarx*) and the sin nature
External enemy: The world (*kosmos*) the systems of greed, lust, and pride
Infernal enemy: The devil (*kakos*) the animating spirit of falsehood and fear

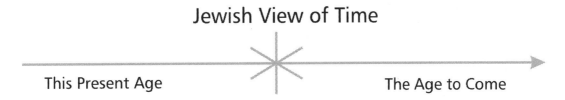

Jewish View of Time

This Present Age — The Age to Come

The Coming of Messiah
The restoration of Israel
The end of Gentile oppression
The return of the earth to Edenic glory
Universal knowledge of the Lord

APPENDIX 12

Jesus of Nazareth: The Presence of the Future

Rev. Dr. Don L. Davis

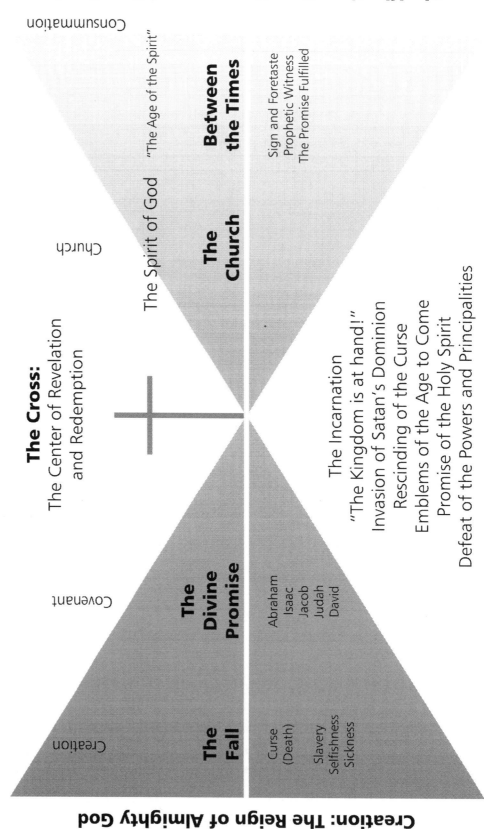

Glorification: New Heavens and New Earth

Consummation

"The Age of the Spirit"

Between the Times

Sign and Foretaste
Prophetic Witness
The Promise Fulfilled

The Spirit of God

Church

The Church

The Cross:
The Center of Revelation
and Redemption

The Incarnation
"The Kingdom is at hand!"
Invasion of Satan's Dominion
Rescinding of the Curse
Emblems of the Age to Come
Promise of the Holy Spirit
Defeat of the Powers and Principalities

The Divine Promise

Covenant

Abraham
Isaac
Jacob
Judah
David

The Fall

Creation

Curse
(Death)

Slavery
Selfishness
Sickness

Creation: The Reign of Almighty God

APPENDIX 13

Traditions

(Paradosis)

Dr. Don L. Davis and Rev. Terry G. Cornett

Strong's Definition

Paradosis. Transmission, i.e. (concretely) a precept; specifically, the Jewish traditionary law

Vine's Explanation

denotes "a tradition," and hence, by metonymy, (a) "the teachings of the rabbis," . . . (b) "apostolic teaching," . . . of instructions concerning the gatherings of believers, of Christian doctrine in general . . . of instructions concerning everyday conduct.

1. **The concept of tradition in Scripture is essentially positive.**

   Jer. 6.16 (ESV) - Thus says the Lord: "Stand by the roads, and look, and ask for the ancient paths, where the good way is; and walk in it, and find rest for your souls. But they said, 'We will not walk in it'" (cf. Exod. 3.15; Judg. 2.17; 1 Kings 8.57-58; Ps. 78.1-6).

   2 Chron. 35.25 (ESV) - Jeremiah also uttered a lament for Josiah; and all the singing men and singing women have spoken of Josiah in their laments to this day. They made these a rule in Israel; behold, they are written in the Laments (cf. Gen. 32.32; Judg. 11.38-40).

   Jer. 35.14-19 (ESV) - The command that Jonadab the son of Rechab gave to his sons, to drink no wine, has been kept, and they drink none to this day, for they have obeyed their father's command. I have spoken to you persistently, but you have not listened to me. I have sent to you all my servants the prophets, sending them persistently, saying, 'Turn now every one of you from his evil way, and amend your deeds, and do not go after other gods to serve them, and then you shall dwell in the land that I gave to you and your fathers.' But you did not incline your ear or listen to me. The sons of Jonadab the son of Rechab have kept the command that their father gave them, but this people has not obeyed me. Therefore, thus says the

Traditions (continued)

Lord, the God of hosts, the God of Israel: Behold, I am bringing upon Judah and all the inhabitants of Jerusalem all the disaster that I have pronounced against them, because I have spoken to them and they have not listened, I have called to them and they have not answered." But to the house of the Rechabites Jeremiah said, "Thus says the Lord of hosts, the God of Israel: Because you have obeyed the command of Jonadab your father and kept all his precepts and done all that he commanded you, therefore thus says the Lord of hosts, the God of Israel: Jonadab the son of Rechab shall never lack a man to stand before me."

2. Godly tradition is a wonderful thing, but not all tradition is godly.

Any individual tradition must be judged by its faithfulness to the Word of God and its usefulness in helping people maintain obedience to Christ's example and teaching.[1] In the Gospels, Jesus frequently rebukes the Pharisees for establishing traditions that nullify rather than uphold God's commands.

Mark 7.8 (ESV) - You leave the commandment of God and hold to the tradition of men" (cf. Matt. 15.2-6; Mark 7.13).

Col. 2.8 (ESV) - See to it that no one takes you captive by philosophy and empty deceit, according to human tradition, according to the elemental spirits of the world, and not according to Christ.

3. Without the fullness of the Holy Spirit, and the constant edification provided to us by the Word of God, tradition will inevitably lead to dead formalism.

Those who are spiritual are filled with the Holy Spirit, whose power and leading alone provides individuals and congregations a sense of freedom and vitality in all they practice and believe. However, when the practices and teachings of any given tradition are no longer infused by the power of the Holy Spirit and the Word of God, tradition loses its effectiveness, and may actually become counterproductive to our discipleship in Jesus Christ.

Eph. 5.18 (ESV) - And do not get drunk with wine, for that is debauchery, but be filled with the Spirit.

[1] "All Protestants insist that these traditions must ever be tested against Scripture and can never possess an independent apostolic authority over or alongside of Scripture." (J. Van Engen, "Tradition," *Evangelical Dictionary of Theology*, Walter Elwell, Gen. ed.) We would add that Scripture is itself the "authoritative tradition" by which all other traditions are judged. See "Appendix A, The Founders of Tradition: Three Levels of Christian Authority," p. 4.

Gal. 5.22-25 (ESV) - But the fruit of the Spirit is love, joy, peace, patience, kindness, goodness, faithfulness, gentleness, self-control; against such things there is no law. And those who belong to Christ Jesus have crucified the flesh with its passions and desires. If we live by the Spirit, let us also walk by the Spirit.

2 Cor. 3.5-6 (ESV) - Not that we are sufficient in ourselves to claim anything as coming from us, but our sufficiency is from God, who has made us competent to be ministers of a new covenant, not of the letter but of the Spirit. For the letter kills, but the Spirit gives life.

4. **Fidelity to the Apostolic Tradition (teaching and modeling) is the essence of Christian maturity.**

2 Tim. 2.2 (ESV) - and what you have heard from me in the presence of many witnesses entrust to faithful men who will be able to teach others also.

1 Cor. 11.1-2 (ESV) - Be imitators of me, as I am of Christ. Now I commend you because you remember me in everything and maintain the traditions even as I delivered them to you (cf.1 Cor. 4.16-17, 2 Tim. 1.13-14, 2 Thess. 3.7-9, Phil. 4.9).

1 Cor. 15.3-8 (ESV) - For I delivered to you as of first importance what I also received: that Christ died for our sins in accordance with the Scriptures, that he was buried, that he was raised on the third day in accordance with the Scriptures, and that he appeared to Cephas, then to the twelve. Then he appeared to more than five hundred brothers at one time, most of whom are still alive, though some have fallen asleep. Then he appeared to James, then to all the apostles. Last of all, as to one untimely born, he appeared also to me.

5. **The Apostle Paul often includes an appeal to the tradition for support in doctrinal practices.**

1 Cor. 11.16 (ESV) - If anyone is inclined to be contentious, we have no such practice, nor do the churches of God (cf. 1 Cor. 1.2, 7.17, 15.3).

Traditions (continued)

> 1 Cor. 14.33-34 (ESV) - For God is not a God of confusion but of peace. As in all the churches of the saints, the women should keep silent in the churches. For they are not permitted to speak, but should be in submission, as the Law also says.

6. When a congregation uses received tradition to remain faithful to the "Word of God," they are commended by the apostles.

> 1 Cor. 11.2 (ESV) - Now I commend you because you remember me in everything and maintain the traditions even as I delivered them to you.

> 2 Thess. 2.15 (ESV) - So then, brothers, stand firm and hold to the traditions that you were taught by us, either by our spoken word or by our letter.

> 2 Thess. 3.6 (ESV) - Now we command you, brothers, in the name of our Lord Jesus Christ, that you keep away from any brother who is walking in idleness and not in accord with the tradition that you received from us.

Appendix A

The Founders of Tradition: Three Levels of Christian Authority

Exod. 3.15 (ESV) - God also said to Moses, "Say this to the people of Israel, 'The Lord, the God of your fathers, the God of Abraham, the God of Isaac, and the God of Jacob, has sent me to you.' This is my name forever, and thus I am to be remembered throughout all generations."

1. The Authoritative Tradition: the Apostles and the Prophets (The Holy Scriptures)

Eph. 2.19-21 (ESV) - So then you are no longer strangers and aliens, but you are fellow citizens with the saints and members of the household of God, built on the foundation of the apostles and prophets, Christ Jesus himself being the cornerstone, in whom the whole structure, being joined together, grows into a holy temple in the Lord.

~ The Apostle Paul

Traditions (continued)

Those who gave eyewitness testimony to the revelation and saving acts of Yahweh, first in Israel, and ultimately in Jesus Christ the Messiah. This testimony is binding for all people, at all times, and in all places. It is the authoritative tradition by which all subsequent tradition is judged.

2. The Great Tradition: the Ecumenical Councils and their Creeds[2]

[2] See Appendix B, "Defining the Great Tradition."

What has been believed everywhere, always, and by all.

~ Vincent of Lerins

The Great Tradition is the core dogma (doctrine) of the Church. It represents the teaching of the Church as it has understood the Authoritative Tradition (the Holy Scriptures), and summarizes those essential truths that Christians of all ages have confessed and believed. To these doctrinal statements the whole Church, (Catholic, Orthodox, and Protestant)[3] gives its assent. The worship and theology of the Church reflects this core dogma, which finds its summation and fulfillment in the person and work of Jesus Christ. From earliest times, Christians have expressed their devotion to God in its Church calendar, a yearly pattern of worship which summarizes and reenacts the events of Christ's life.

[3] Even the more radical wing of the Protestant reformation (Anabaptists) who were the most reluctant to embrace the creeds as dogmatic instruments of faith, did not disagree with the essential content found in them. "They assumed the Apostolic Creed–they called it 'The Faith,' **Der Glaube**, as did most people." See John Howard Yoder, **Preface to Theology: Christology and Theological Method.** Grand Rapids: Brazos Press, 2002. pp. 222-223.

3. Specific Church Traditions: the Founders of Denominations and Orders

The Presbyterian Church (U.S.A.) has approximately 2.5 million members, 11,200 congregations and 21,000 ordained ministers. Presbyterians trace their history to the 16th century and the Protestant Reformation. Our heritage, and much of what we believe, began with the French lawyer John Calvin (1509-1564), whose writings crystallized much of the Reformed thinking that came before him.

~ The Presbyterian Church, U.S.A.

Christians have expressed their faith in Jesus Christ in various ways through specific movements and traditions which embrace and express the Authoritative Tradition and the Great Tradition in unique ways. For instance,

Traditions (continued)

Catholic movements have arisen around people like Benedict, Francis, or Dominic, and among Protestants people like Martin Luther, John Calvin, Ulrich Zwingli, and John Wesley. Women have founded vital movements of Christian faith (e.g., Aimee Semple McPherson of the Foursquare Church), as well as minorities (e.g., Richard Allen of the African Methodist Episcopal Church or Charles H. Mason of the Church of God in Christ, who also helped to spawn the Assemblies of God), all which attempted to express the Authoritative Tradition and the Great Tradition in a specific way consistent with their time and expression.

The emergence of vital, dynamic movements of the faith at different times and among different peoples reveal the fresh working of the Holy Spirit throughout history. Thus, inside Catholicism, new communities have arisen such as the Benedictines, Franciscans, and Dominicans; and outside Catholicism, new denominations have emerged (Lutherans, Presbyterians, Methodists, Church of God in Christ, etc.). Each of these specific traditions have "founders," key leaders whose energy and vision helped to establish a unique expression of Christian faith and practice. Of course, to be legitimate, these movements must adhere to and faithfully express both the Authoritative Tradition and the Great Tradition. Members of these specific traditions embrace their own unique practices and patterns of spirituality, but these unique features are not necessarily binding on the Church at large. They represent the unique expressions of that community's understanding of and faithfulness to the Authoritative and Great Traditions.

Specific traditions seek to express and live out this faithfulness to the Authoritative and Great Traditions through their worship, teaching, and service. They seek to make the Gospel clear within new cultures or sub-cultures, speaking and modeling the hope of Christ into new situations shaped by their own set of questions posed in light of their own unique circumstances. These movements, therefore, seek to contextualize the Authoritative tradition in a way that faithfully and effectively leads new groups of people to faith in Jesus Christ, and incorporates those who believe into the community of faith that obeys his teachings and gives witness of him to others.

Appendix B

Defining the "Great Tradition"

The Great Tradition (sometimes called the "classical Christian tradition") is defined by Robert E. Webber as follows:

> *[It is] the broad outline of Christian belief and practice developed from the Scriptures between the time of Christ and the middle of the fifth century*

> ~ Webber. **The Majestic Tapestry**.
> Nashville: Thomas Nelson Publishers, 1986. p. 10.

This tradition is widely affirmed by Protestant theologians both ancient and modern.

> *Thus those ancient Councils of Nicea, Constantinople, the first of Ephesus, Chalcedon, and the like, which were held for refuting errors, we willingly embrace, and reverence as sacred, in so far as relates to doctrines of faith, for they contain nothing but the pure and genuine interpretation of Scripture, which the holy Fathers with spiritual prudence adopted to crush the enemies of religion who had then arisen.*

> ~ John Calvin. **Institutes**. IV, ix. 8.

> *. . . most of what is enduringly valuable in contemporary biblical exegesis was discovered by the fifth century.*

> ~ Thomas C. Oden. **The Word of Life**.
> San Francisco: HarperSanFrancisco, 1989. p. xi

> *The first four Councils are by far the most important, as they settled the orthodox faith on the Trinity and the Incarnation.*

> ~ Philip Schaff. **The Creeds of Christendom**. Vol. 1.
> Grand Rapids: Baker Book House, 1996. p. 44.

Our reference to the Ecumenical Councils and Creeds is, therefore, focused on those Councils which retain a widespread agreement in the Church among Catholics, Orthodox, and Protestants. While Catholic and Orthodox share common agreement on the first seven councils, Protestants tend to affirm and use primarily the first four. Therefore, those councils which continue to be shared by the whole Church are completed with the Council of Chalcedon in 451.

Traditions (continued)

It is worth noting that each of these four Ecumenical Councils took place in a pre-European cultural context and that none of them were held in Europe. They were councils of the whole Church and they reflected a time in which Christianity was primarily an eastern religion in it's geographic core. By modern reckoning, their participants were African, Asian, and European. The councils reflected a church that ". . . has roots in cultures far distant from Europe and preceded the development of modern European identity, and [of which] some of its greatest minds have been African" (Oden, *The Living God*, San Francisco: HarperSanFrancisco, 1987, p. 9).

Perhaps the most important achievement of the Councils was the creation of what is now commonly called the Nicene Creed. It serves as a summary statement of the Christian faith that can be agreed on by Catholic, Orthodox, and Protestant Christians.

The first four Ecumenical Councils are summarized in the following chart:

Name/Date/Location	Purpose
First Ecumenical Council 325 A.D. Nicea, Asia Minor	Defending against: *Arianism* Question answered: *Was Jesus God?* Action: *Developed the initial form of the Nicene Creed to serve as a summary of the Christian faith*
Second Ecumenical Council 381 A.D. Constantinople, Asia Minor	Defending against: *Macedonianism* Question answered: *Is the Holy Spirit a personal and equal part of the Godhead?* Action: *Completed the Nicene Creed by expanding the article dealing with the Holy Spirit*
Third Ecumenical Council 431 A.D. Ephesus, Asia Minor	Defending against: *Nestorianism* Question answered: *Is Jesus Christ both God and man in one person?* Action: *Defined Christ as the Incarnate Word of God and affirmed his mother Mary as* **theotokos** *(God-bearer)*
Fourth Ecumenical Council 451 A.D. Chalcedon, Asia Minor	Defending against: *Monophysitism* Question answered: *How can Jesus be both God and man?* Action: *Explained the relationship between Jesus' two natures (human and Divine)*

APPENDIX 14

Fit to Represent

Multiplying Disciples of the Kingdom of God

Rev. Dr. Don L. Davis · Luke 10.16 (ESV) - The one who hears you hears me, and the one who rejects you rejects me, and the one who rejects me rejects him who sent me.

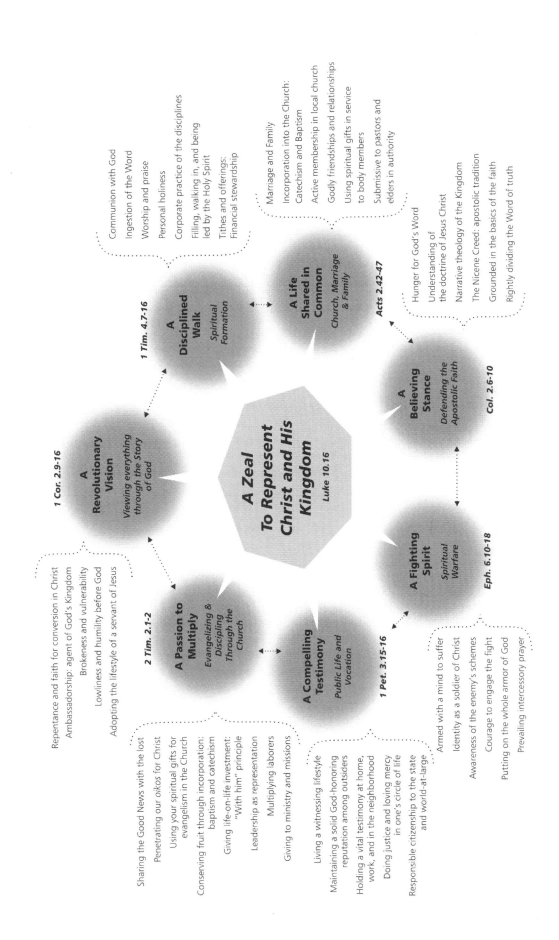

A Zeal To Represent Christ and His Kingdom
Luke 10.16

A Disciplined Walk
Spiritual Formation
1 Tim. 4.7-16

- Communion with God
- Ingestion of the Word
- Worship and praise
- Personal holiness
- Corporate practice of the disciplines
- Filling, walking in, and being led by the Holy Spirit
- Tithes and offerings: Financial stewardship

A Life Shared in Common
Church, Marriage & Family
Acts 2.42-47

- Marriage and Family
- Incorporation into the Church: Catechism and Baptism
- Active membership in local church
- Godly friendships and relationships
- Using spiritual gifts in service to body members
- Submissive to pastors and elders in authority

A Believing Stance
Defending the Apostolic Faith
Col. 2.6-10

- Hunger for God's Word
- Understanding of the doctrine of Jesus Christ
- Narrative theology of the Kingdom
- The Nicene Creed: apostolic tradition
- Grounded in the basics of the faith
- Rightly dividing the Word of truth

A Fighting Spirit
Spiritual Warfare
Eph. 6.10-18

- Armed with a mind to suffer
- Identity as a soldier of Christ
- Awareness of the enemy's schemes
- Courage to engage the fight
- Putting on the whole armor of God
- Prevailing intercessory prayer

A Compelling Testimony
Public Life and Vocation
1 Pet. 3.15-16

- Living a witnessing lifestyle
- Maintaining a solid God-honoring reputation among outsiders
- Holding a vital testimony at home, work, and in the neighborhood
- Doing justice and loving mercy in one's circle of life
- Responsible citizenship to the state and world-at-large

A Passion to Multiply
Evangelizing & Discipling Through the Church
2 Tim. 2.1-2

- Sharing the Good News with the lost
- Penetrating our *oikos* for Christ
- Using your spiritual gifts for evangelism in the Church
- Conserving fruit through incorporation: baptism and catechism
- Giving life-on-life investment: "With him" principle
- Leadership as representation
- Multiplying laborers
- Giving to ministry and missions

A Revolutionary Vision
Viewing everything through the Story of God
1 Cor. 2.9-16

- Repentance and faith for conversion in Christ
- Ambassadorship: agent of God's Kingdom
- Brokenness and vulnerability
- Lowliness and humility before God
- Adopting the lifestyle of a servant of Jesus

APPENDIX 15

The *Oikos* Factor

Spheres of Relationship and Influence

Rev. Dr. Don L. Davis

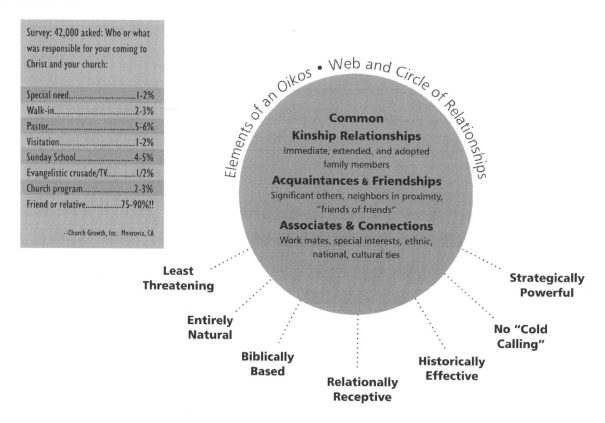

Survey: 42,000 asked: Who or what was responsible for your coming to Christ and your church:

Special need	1-2%
Walk-in	2-3%
Pastor	5-6%
Visitation	1-2%
Sunday School	4-5%
Evangelistic crusade/TV	1/2%
Church program	2-3%
Friend or relative	75-90%!!

--Church Growth, Inc. Monrovia, CA

Elements of an Oikos • Web and Circle of Relationships

Common Kinship Relationships
Immediate, extended, and adopted family members

Acquaintances & Friendships
Significant others, neighbors in proximity, "friends of friends"

Associates & Connections
Work mates, special interests, ethnic, national, cultural ties

Least Threatening

Entirely Natural

Biblically Based

Relationally Receptive

Historically Effective

No "Cold Calling"

Strategically Powerful

Oikos (household) in the OT

"A household usually contained four generations, including men, married women, unmarried daughters, slaves of both sexes, persons without citizenship, and "sojourners," or resident foreign workers." – *Hans Walter Wolff, Anthology of the Old Testament.*

Oikos (household) in the NT

Evangelism and disciple making in our NT narratives are often described as following the flow of the relational networks of various people within their *oikoi* (households), that is, those natural lines of connection in which they resided and lived (c.f., Mark 5.19; Luke 19.9; John 4.53; 1.41-45, etc.). Andrew to Simon (John 1.41-45), and both Cornelius (Acts 10-11) and the Philippian jailer (Acts 16) are notable cases of evangelism and discipling through *oikoi*.

Oikos (household) among the urban poor

While great differences exist between cultures, kinship relationships, special interest groups, and family structures among urban populations, it is clear that urbanites connect with others far more on the basis of connections through relationships, friendships, and family than through proximity and neighborhood alone. Often times the closest friends of urban poor dwellers are not immediately close-by in terms of neighborhood; family and friends may dwell blocks, even miles away. Taking the time to study the precise linkages of relationships among the dwellers in a certain area can prove extremely helpful in determining the most effective strategies for evangelism and disciple making in inner city contexts.

APPENDIX 16

Receptivity Scale

The Holmes-Rahe Social Readjustment Scale indicates different events, in approximate order of their importance, that have an effect in producing periods of personal or family transition. The numbers on the right indicate the importance of the event relative to other transition-producing events. Various events may compound each other when an individual experiences more than one incident over a relatively short period of time. The higher the number, the more receptive the person is to the Gospel. For example, someone who was just married and is also having trouble with his or her boss will be more receptive than if either event had occurred separately. Also, the larger the number or accumulation of numbers, the longer the period of transition will last and the more intense it will be.

~ Win Arn and Charles Arn.
The Master's Plan for Making Disciples. 2nd ed.
Grand Rapids: Baker Books, 1998.
pp. 88-89

The Holmes-Rahe Social Readjustment Scale

Event	Value
Death of Spouse	100
Divorce	73
Marital Separation	65
Jail Term	63
Death of Close Family Member	63
Personal Injury or Illness	53
Marriage	50
Fired from Work	47
Marital Reconciliation	45
Retirement	45
Change in Family Member's Health	44
Pregnancy	40
Sex Difficulties	39
Addition to Family	39
Business Readjustment	39
Change in Financial Status	38
Death of Close Friend	37
Change in Number of Marital Arguments	35
Mortgage or Loan over $75,000	31
Foreclosure of Mortgage or Loan	30
Change in Work Responsibilities	29
Son or Daughter Leaving Home	29
Trouble with In-Laws	29
Outstanding Personal Achievement	28
Spouse Starts Work	26
Starting or Finishing School	26
Change in Living Conditions	25
Revision of Personal Habits	24
Trouble with Boss	23
Change in Work Hours or Conditions	20
Change in Residence	20
Change in Schools	20
Change in Recreational Habits	19
Change in Social Activities	18
Mortgage or Loan under $75,000	18
Easter Season	17
Change in Sleeping Habits	16
Change in Number of Family Gatherings	15
Vacation	13
Christmas Season	12
Minor Violation of the Law	11

APPENDIX 17

Relationship of Cost and Effectiveness in Disciple-Making Endeavors

Taken from Win Arn and Charles Arn, **The Master's Plan for Making Disciples**. *2nd ed. Grand Rapids: Baker Books, 1998. pp. 166*

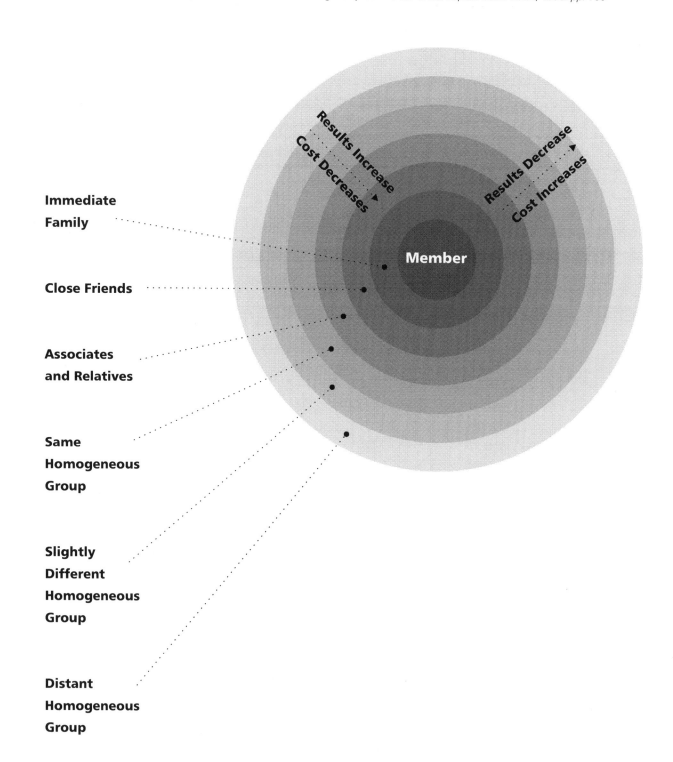

Immediate
Family

Close Friends

Associates
and Relatives

Same
Homogeneous
Group

Slightly
Different
Homogeneous
Group

Distant
Homogeneous
Group

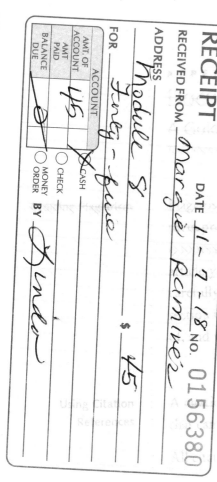

1 8

nting Your Work

Help You Give Credit Where Credit Is Due

Institute

using another person's ideas as if they belonged to you without giving credit. In academic work it is just as wrong to steal a person's ideas as it erson's property. These ideas may come from the author of a book, an ave read, or from a fellow student. The way to avoid plagiarism is to "notes" (textnotes, footnotes, endnotes, etc.) and a "Works Cited" lp people who read your work know when an idea is one you thought you are borrowing an idea from another person.

eference is required in a paper whenever you use ideas or information rom another person's work.

references involve two parts:

tes in the body of your paper placed next to each quotation which came from an outside source.

- A "Works Cited" page at the end of your paper or project which gives information about the sources you have used

Using Notes in Your Paper

There are three basic kinds of notes: parenthetical notes, footnotes, and endnotes. At The Urban Ministry Institute, we recommend that students use parenthetical notes. These notes give the author's last name(s), the date the book was published, and the page number(s) on which you found the information. Example:

In trying to understand the meaning of Genesis 14.1-24, it is important to recognize that in biblical stories "the place where dialogue is first introduced will be an important moment in revealing the character of the speaker . . ." (Kaiser and Silva 1994, 73). This is certainly true of the character of Melchizedek who speaks words of blessing. This identification of Melchizedek as a positive spiritual influence is reinforced by the fact that he is the King of Salem, since Salem means "safe, at peace" (Wiseman 1996, 1045).

Documenting Your Work (continued)

A "Works Cited" page should be placed at the end of your paper. This page:

Creating a Works
Cited Page

- lists every source you quoted in your paper

- is in alphabetical order by author's last name

- includes the date of publication and information about the publisher

The following formatting rules should be followed:

1. Title

The title "Works Cited" should be used and centered on the first line of the page following the top margin.

2. Content

Each reference should list:

- the author's full name (last name first)

- the date of publication

- the title and any special information (Revised edition, 2nd edition, reprint) taken from the cover or title page should be noted

- the city where the publisher is headquartered followed by a colon and the name of the publisher

3. Basic form

- Each piece of information should be separated by a period.

- The second line of a reference (and all following lines) should be indented.

- Book titles should be underlined (or italicized).

- Article titles should be placed in quotes.

Example:

Fee, Gordon D. 1991. *Gospel and Spirit: Issues in New Testament Hermeneutics.* Peabody, MA: Hendrickson Publishers.

Documenting Your Work (continued)

4. Special Forms

A book with multiple authors:

> Kaiser, Walter C., and Moisés Silva. 1994. *An Introduction to Biblical Hermeneutics: The Search for Meaning.* Grand Rapids: Zondervan Publishing House.

An edited book:

> Greenway, Roger S., ed. 1992. *Discipling the City: A Comprehensive Approach to Urban Mission.* 2nd ed. Grand Rapids: Baker Book House.

A book that is part of a series:

> Morris, Leon. 1971. *The Gospel According to John.* Grand Rapids: Wm. B. Eerdmans Publishing Co. The New International Commentary on the New Testament. Gen. ed. F. F. Bruce.

An article in a reference book:

> Wiseman, D. J. "Salem." 1982. In *New Bible Dictionary.* Leicester, England - Downers Grove, IL: InterVarsity Press. Eds. I. H. Marshall and others.

(An example of a "Works Cited" page is located on the next page.)

For Further Research

Standard guides to documenting academic work in the areas of philosophy, religion, theology, and ethics include:

> Atchert, Walter S., and Joseph Gibaldi. 1985. *The MLA Style Manual.* New York: Modern Language Association.

> *The Chicago Manual of Style.* 1993. 14th ed. Chicago: The University of Chicago Press.

> Turabian, Kate L. 1987. *A Manual for Writers of Term Papers, Theses, and Dissertations.* 5th edition. Bonnie Bertwistle Honigsblum, ed. Chicago: The University of Chicago Press.

Documenting Your Work (continued)

Works Cited

Fee, Gordon D. 1991. *Gospel and Spirit: Issues in New Testament Hermeneutics*. Peabody, MA: Hendrickson Publishers.

Greenway, Roger S., ed. 1992. *Discipling the City: A Comprehensive Approach to Urban Mission*. 2nd ed. Grand Rapids: Baker Book House.

Kaiser, Walter C., and Moisés Silva. 1994. *An Introduction to Biblical Hermeneutics: The Search for Meaning*. Grand Rapids: Zondervan Publishing House.

Morris, Leon. 1971. *The Gospel According to John*. Grand Rapids: Wm. B. Eerdmans Publishing Co. *The New International Commentary on the New Testament*. Gen. ed. F. F. Bruce.

Wiseman, D. J. "Salem." 1982. In *New Bible Dictionary*. Leicester, England-Downers Grove, IL: InterVarsity Press. Eds. I. H. Marshall and others.

Made in the USA
Columbia, SC
24 October 2018